Abul Hasan Ali An-Nadwi

A man of hope through
a century of turmoil

Syed Iqbal Zaheer

Dar ul Thaqafah
www.darulthaqafah.com
https://twitter.com/darulthaqafah

Find our titles on your favorite online bookstore using the keyword 'Dar Ul Thaqafah'.

2023 CE – 1444 H

Translation of the Qur'ān

It should be perfectly clear that the Qur'ān is only authentic in its original language, Arabic. Since perfect translation of the Qur'ān is impossible, we have used the translation of the meaning of the Qur'ān throughout the book, as the result is only a crude meaning of the Arabic text.

Qur'ānic verses appear in speech marks proceeded by a reference to the Surah and verse number. Sayings (*Hadith*) of Prophet Muhammad (saw) appear in inverted commas along with reference to the Hadith Book and its Reporter.

Contents

Foreword 7
Early Life 9
    Background 9
    Childhood 10
    Arabic, Urdu and other Studies 11
    At Lahore 13
    Scholars and Shuyukh of the Time 16
    First Few Writings 20
    At Deoband 21
Adulthood 23
    A Teacher 23
    The First Book 24
    Way Apart 28
    Tablighee Jama`at 33
    Maa Dha 35
    To the Elite 40
    A Charged Atmosphere 42
    In Egypt 45
    Change of Heart? 46

Saviors of Islamic Spirit	49
The New Apostasy	51
Nadwah's Rector	53
Riots at Home	55
The 1967 Debacle	59
Uniform Civil Code	63
Majlis-e-Mushawarat	68
Payam-e-Insaniyyat	70
Vande Mataram	73
Late Years	74
The Faisal Award	74
Oxford University	77
In Yemen	80
Shah Waliyullah	82
Shah Banu Case	83
Muslim Women	85
Sati	87
The Gulf War	89
Another Letter	90
The Babari Masjid	91
Payam-e-Insaniyyat Again	95

- A few other Responses 96
- A Long Journey 99
- The Divisionary Forces 104
- Vande Mataram Again 107

His Person 116
- Personal Habits 116
- Quality of Speech and Writings 118
- Asceticism 123
- Standing Among the Scholars 128

The Last Days and Death 132

Foreword

This writer did not have the honor of an intimate relationship with the personality whose biography this is. In fact, the opportunity to spend a couple of hours with him also did not arise but perhaps once, at Nadwah, in the nineties. We lived in worlds apart, and overwhelming engagements of both – at of course different level of activities – prevented frequent contacts. If it is said that personal acquaintance was anything but casual, it would not be wrong. I knew him primarily through his books, articles and speeches that appeared at a regular pace in the Muslim press. He was one of those whose writings were awaited, especially during his late years, when no other scholar of his caliber - of a caravan that had moved out - was left behind. Ali Miyan too knew this writer through some of his books, two of which he had embellished with his foreword. He was also the general supervisor of Young Muslim Digest magazine, whose editorship has been this writer's responsibility almost since its inception.

This writer then is not qualified in any particular way to write his biography. But, firstly, a good one, preferably by a close associate, is yet to appear. The days of "*qaht al-rijal*" are, apparently, behind us; we seem now to have entered into the final phase of "*fiqd al-rijal*." Secondly, a series of articles by this writer on his life had already appeared in the above-mentioned magazine. Although a bit haphazard, and quite inadequate for several reasons, and therefore, not at all befitting a personality whose imprints can be seen both in literature, as well as in individual personalities, yet it seemed appropriate that they should be put together and brought out as a book to meet with the requirements of the general public until a larger and more satisfying work appears.

This little book then, is no tribute to him. It deserves the apology that these lines express. But, as they say in Arabic, "if the whole cannot be captured, the essence may not be relinquished."

Syed Iqbal Zaheer
Bangalore
July, 2005

Early Life

Background

Some seventy km off Lucknow (capital of Uttar Pradesh - India), lies a district in the north-west called Rae Bareli. A narrow winding path on the north-eastern flank of the town, across the agricultural fields, meadows and shrubs, insects and surprise birds, leads to a small village whose size suggests the nomenclature of a settlement rather than a village. Once somewhat more populous, now it boasts of some 8-10 houses. The village was established by the famous Shah `Ilm-u-Allah Hasani, Naqshbandi, in the 17th century. Atop a raised area, you could walk down the end of the village some distance across a slopy field to reach the bank of the quiet river Sayyi. Occasionally, maybe twice or thrice a century, the river swells and threatens to swallow the village.

At such times its inhabitants run for their life along with the precious load of books from the fairly well-equipped village library. Amidst the old and new houses, a mosque stands tall - a little less taller though, than the Ka`bah on whose pattern it has been built. It has no minarets. Two huge tamarind trees stand at both ends of the village as if on guard. The village cemetery, a short distance away - bereft of tombs, epitaphs, or plastered humps - is almost entirely composed of the extended family, sleeping next to each other peacefully, spared the throng of visitors, although many were *Awliya' Allah* in their own right in their own time. Called *Takyaa Kalaan*, it is here in this small village that several generations of scholars, sufis, *mujahids*, *masha ikh*, poets, historians and men of renown appeared, grew and spread around to reach out the masses over wide areas. Sayyid Abul Hasan Ali al-Nadwi (Ali Miyan of later times) was one of them. This is where he was born some 90 years ago. This is where he sought recluse after every hectic activity that took him thousands of miles away from his ancestral home.

Childhood

Born in the same year as Shibli died (1914), to a quiet, hard-working, scholarly father and a very religious mother (who wouldn't let the child miss a single prayer), he was tutored, following the custom of the time, by scholars of sorts, spending most of his childhood in Lucknow where Abdul Hayy, his father ran a clinic. Abdul Hayy, author of the 8 volume Arabic *Nuzhatu al-Khawatir*, and several works in Urdu, was also the rector of the Nadwatul 'Ulama (popularly, the Nadwah), a traditional type of *Madrasah* with modernistic leanings.

In his childhood, Ali Miyan spent a few hours studying Qur'an in the traditional *Maktab* of the local mosque where he finished his first Qur'an-reading. Later, roughly from the age of seven, various teachers took charge. He was put on a variety of study courses in Urdu, English, Persian, Arabic. Those days masters assessed every child's capacities and aptitudes and taught him books most suitable to him. An intelligent child, for example, did not follow the rigmarole of the average students.

His elder brother Abdul Ali - from his father's earlier marriage - had done his preliminary course at Nadwah, advanced courses at Deoband, and had then got himself enrolled for a degree in medicine at the Lucknow University. After completion of the course and practice for a few years, he was to abandon the allopathic for the homeopathic, although at the cost of well-to-do patients and their purses. In fact, the family tried a few books of medicine on Ali also, but for lack of interest on his part, they gave up.

He lost his father at the age of nine. Massaging his feet, the child hardly realized the peaceful transition of the father into the next world. After him, the family couldn't afford to live in the rented house at Lucknow and had to shift back to the modest Takiya Kalan where the child continued to take lessons in Persian from one of his uncles. Soon, however, thanks to the support of some well-wishers, the family shifted back to Lucknow under the charge of the elder son of the family who was continuing his medical studies at the Lucknow University.

Arabic, Urdu and other Studies

Ali Miyan was entrusted for his Arabic language to a private but unpaid tutorship (Indian scholars never charged a fee for their services), of Sheikh Khalil ibn Muhammad. Originally a Yemeni and at that time professor in the Arabic language at the Lucknow

University, he was a teacher of his own class. Following a self-designed syllabus he took his students across miles in weeks. Ali Miyan studied several years under this skillful teacher. One of those days he was introduced to Zakir Hussain Khan (later, President of India), who, fresh from Germany with a doctorate degree, was pleasantly surprised at hearing a young lad speak in unbroken Arabic.

In Urdu he received some coaching from an elder cousin, Hafiz Sayyid Habibur Rahman, who was studying at Jami`a Milliyah. Writings of Azaad (Bilgirami), Shibli, Haali, (Deputy) Nazeer Ahmed, Sharar, Ratan Nath Sarshaar and a few other leading writers, not to forget his own father's works, formed the core of his studies in those days of quick and lasting impression.

Also, during those days, the famous Qur'an scholar and commentator Khwajah Abdul Hayy visited the family. Ali Miyan's brother Abdul Ali ordered him to do a quick course with him. Khawjah had a unique style and his coaching helped Ali Miyan qualify for attendance to another Qur'anic course conducted by Ahmed Ali Lahori, at Labore, a thousand miles away. However, before he could go there, he was fortunate enough to study Arabic grammar under the famous grammarian Sayyid Talha.

When he was 13 he was advised to enroll himself at the Lucknow University for an advanced study course in the Arabic language. He was the youngest to appear in the entrance test, but emerged at top in order of merit. In two years time he completed the Senior Level course obtaining a gold medal for topping the class, thanks to the strong foundation that Sheikh Khalil and Sayyid Talha had provided him. The gold medal also earned him a scholarship for a year which he spent at the university doing a special course in *Hadith*. But, as he wrote later, he was mortified that the *Hadith* degree was presented to him by an unbelieving British Governor, Sir Malcolm Haley. He couldn't forget the distastefulness even after the lapse of half a century.

His elder brother was a disciple of Hussain Ahmed Madani, a *Hadith* scholar, Sufi, and a freedom fighter who had spent several years in Andaman Islands along with his mentor Mahmoodul Hasan, the *Sheikh al-Hind*. They were imprisoned in the island by the British. Abdul Ali was so close to Hussain Ahmed Madani that whenever the latter came to Lucknow, and it was not unoften that he did, he stayed in his house. So, for days and weeks of those early impressionable days, the lad Ali spent time with the great Sheikh. The Sheikh possessed a very attractive personality and was second to none in scholarship after his own master the *Sheikh al-Hind*.

At Lahore

Ali was now 15 and traveled to Lahore where he was advised by a professor - who saw some of his Arabic writings including a translation of Dr. Iqbal's "*Chana*" in Arabic prose - to specialize in Arabic literature. He returned however, to become, on the behest of his brother, a pupil of *Hadith* under the famous *Sheikh al-Hadith*

Hayder Hasan Khan at Nadwah. Under him he studied Bukhari, Muslim, Tirmidhi and Abu Da'ud. The course included not only the text, which was read by the students before the Sheikh, word by word, but also details of the narrators, their (or textual) weaknesses, finer technical details, etc. The Sheikh also trained his students in research work. That was followed by a course in *Fiqh*, taught by the famous specialist Mawlana Shibli Jirajpuri.

To give an idea of the quality of students around the young Ali Miyan, we might mention the names of Mas'ud 'Aalam, Abdul Quddus Hashmi (Karachi), Abdus Salam Qidwai, Muhammad Nazim, Muhibbullah (vice-chancellor, Nadwah), Hafiz Abdus Shakoor, Muhammad Uways (*Sheikh al-Tafsir* at Nadwah), Muhammad 'Imran Khan (who built the famous Bhopal mosque), Ra'is Ahmed Ja'feri, (the novelist) Muhammad Nazim (vice-chancellor Nadwah), and several others who outshined each other as Ali's Nadwah colleagues.

As providence should have it, he had not completed his *Hadith* studies at Nadwah when Taqiuddin Hilali, the famous Arabic linguist arrived in India. He was an expert in the Arabic language and a personality of such caliber that when giants like Rashid Rida (Egypt) and Ameer Shakeeb Arsalaan (Syria) - two leading and the most influential scholars of the Muslim world of that time – clashed over a grammar point, he acted as the arbiter and judge. On the run because of some political problems back home, he tried to settle down in India. He was so well-known the world over that the Arabic language teachers flocked around him to sort out grammar issues. Ali Miyan became his student, to study the language for full two years. Under this skillful teacher he covered the long and difficult road to proficiency in Arabic language in leaps and bounds.

It may be pointed out at this juncture, that in addition to the fact that those were days of knowledge, when the "run of the mill" scholars in India knew more than perhaps the self-proclaimed *mujtahids* of today, there were two factors that helped Ali Miyan become what he became. First, his family was composed of scholars, *Shuyukh*, and other distinguished figures. Devoted to religion, the thoughts of getting a fair share of this world never crossed their minds. His father had by his own choice discontinued to receive salary from the Nadwah, depending entirely on his practice. An author of several books, he didn't even get his 8-volume *Nuzhatul Khawatir* (which has the biography of four thousand and five hundred scholars and renowned men of India), printed in his life. Ali Miyan's brother, Abdul Ali gave up practicing allopathic medicine despite heavy financial loss. So, the family knew what a child was to do and how to go about achieving the objectives of life, whatever the material conditions. The objectives themselves were clearly defined: knowledge and service. Little else mattered. In the face of these objectives set by the family, friends, elders and the society, the need for admonition or discipline did not arise. Secondly, it was never difficult for the family to convince any top order teacher to accept one of it members for coaching because of the respect the family enjoyed for its scholarly achievements. Consequently, given Ali Miyan's own abilities, coupled with Divine

Favor, it wasn't for any of his teachers to lament the loss of his useful time. They knew what fruits their efforts would bear and offered their best to a hungry soul.

Scholars and Shuyukh of the Time

Luckily, as we have said earlier, and in view of the adage that a man is what his teachers and the social milieu make of him, those were days when eminent men were available for the asking. They were not merely men of letters. They were practitioners of the spirit that underscored the written word. Men like Hussain Ahmed Madani (*Hadith*), Ahmed Ali Lahori (the Master of masters in Qur'anic studies), Taqiuddin Hilali (the linguist), Dr. Sir Muhammad Iqbal (the poet), Habibur Rahman Khan Sherwani, Abul Kalam Azad (the man of letters), Ashraf Ali Thanwi (the Alusi of India), Prof. Ilyas Burni, Dr. Sir Ziyauddin, Khalil b. Ahmed (the grammarian), Hayder Hussain Khan (*Sheikh al-Hadith*), Manazir Ahsan Geelani (author of the unique work *Khatam un-Nabiyyin*), 'Abdul Bari Nadwi, 'Ubaydullah Sindhi, Abdul Majid Daryabadi (the *Majma' al-Bahrayn* of India who had the distinction of writing two Qur'anic commentaries: in Urdu and English) Mawlana Zakariyyah Kandhlawi (*Sheikh al-Hadith* - the great populizer of *Hadith* among the masses), Sa'id Ahmed Akbar Abadi (*Life of Abu Bakr*), Sayyid Sulayman Nadwi (the all-round scholar *par excellence*), Shabbir Ahmed 'Uthmani (*Tafsir-e-'Uthmani*), Mawlana 'Abdul Qadir Ra'epuri (the *Sufi*), Mawlana Ilyas Ahmed (the great *Da'ee*) and many others who excelled in their special fields - were within easy reach of any serious student.

In fact, such was the quality and so large the galaxy of scholars at the end of the 19th century and the first quarter of the 20th century in India, that students and scholars from all parts of the Islamic world were constantly arriving to either pursue higher studies or seek employment in their field of specialization. Ali Miyan did not finish with one but to take position with another giant, all about ready to incarnate himself into the young, studious, impressionable and extremely pliant lad.

Not only these scholars, spiritualists, intellectuals and *Shuyukh* trained and guided him on day to day basis, but they also earnestly prayed for him in their supplications. He was an extremely likeable person because of his amiability and was universally looked upon as someone in the making, on whom they could fasten their hopes. In fact, even in his later life, most of his affairs in connection with journeys, *Da`wah* works, articles, books or teaching jobs were decided in consultation with or by the urging of his mentors. His activities had their backing, won full blessing, and drew a few supplications. When he spoke, or wrote, they were the first to congratulate him and encourage him to further tasks. In this sense he stood truly distinct: there was not a well-known scholar or religious personality throughout the length and breadth of India but from whom he had not drawn some fuel for his spiritual lantern.

A single incident will say a lot about the kind of discipline, teacher-student relationship, and the general miliue that was prevalent among the learned of those days. One day when the English teacher knocked at the door, Ali Miyan emerged to tell him that he would not be able to take lessons for some reason or the other. That granted, the lad closed the door, a bit hard, which sounded like he had slammed it against the teacher. The teacher felt affronted. He complained to Ali's Arabic teacher, the Yemeni Sheikh Khalil. Sheikh Khalil spoke to `Ali's elder brother and guardian Abdul `Ali and let him know that he was going to spank the lad. When Ali showed up, he gave him a thrashing that put Ali in a sort of bad shape. When Ali went to his village Takyaa Kalaan his mother asked, "So you were spanked by Sheikh Khalil? Were you? What went wrong?" The lad explained the misunderstanding and kind of defended the teacher.

What has to be noted is that nobody interfered, nobody commented and nobody protested. The mother too did not say a word about her dear child or the teacher who spanked. Obviously, had anything of that kind happened, the lad would have had to do not only without those teachers, but many others.

Otherwise of course, the teachers, scholars and others were absolutely sincere people. They looked at a lad as to what they could make of him, if he was willing to follow the course suggested by them. Their love for their pupils was immense. They would go any length to remove a pupil's doubt during the course or after it. They'd never refuse to teach anyone who showed the inclination to learn. They worked during their vacations, at no cost. In fact, in some cases they spent their own money on a deserving student. When a student distinguished himself in some way, they went about speaking proudly of him in their assemblies, guiding him to further courses, writing strong letters of recommendation, and then following up the matter with the next batch of teachers. At night they earnestly prayed for their pupils.

A few incidents might throw more light on the culture of the religious class of those times. When Mawlana Ashraf Ali Thanwi received a copy of Ali Miyan's "*Seerat Sayyid Ahmed Shahia*," he kissed the book after opening the parcel. Then, as he scanned it, he hugged it and involuntarily raising his hands began to supplicate for the author, with the disciples around him chanting *Ameen*. When in the year 1975, under the rectorship of Ali Miyan, Nadwah was celebrating its Golden Jubilee, having served the community for eighty-five years, Sheikh Zakariyyah Kandhlawi sent a few of his disciples to pitch their tent near the venue and engage themselves in nothing but unbroken supplications for the success of the function!

And once `Abdul Qadir Ra'epuri - moved by his "state" - suddenly said, "I am going to supplicate for Ali Miyan. All of you [the disciples] will say *Ameen*!" On another occasion, Ali Miyan was passing by Bhopal. He wrote to his his Sheikh - Mawlana Ya`qub Bhopali - that against his usual habit of breaking the train journey to meet him, he wouldn't be stepping down this time since the train would be reaching the town at mid-night. The train was late by two hours, but when Ali Miyan looked out of the window, he found his Sheikh standing on the platform shivering in severe cold along with a few disciples. Ali Miyan pooled up courage to say that the Sheikh had troubled himself. The reply was, "I have never enjoyed an occasion like I enjoyed it today." The two parted with an embrace and said goodbye with moistened eyes.

At all events, it might be pointed out that such were not the attitudes of the *Shuyukh* specifically with Ali Miyan. Where there was spiritual, or even intellectual talent, such were the ways of the *Shuyukh* of the Indian sub-continent of that historic period.

First Few Writings

Trained by such able teachers, guided by such eminent scholars, paces set by such preeminent *Shuyukh*, supplicated for by such powerful souls, (not to forget his mother, the tireless supplicator, come morning, come evening, come *tahajjud*, come Friday), and helped on by his own consistent efforts, Ali Miyan soon began to produce articles of worth in the Urdu and Arabic languages. The first notable one was on the life of Sayyid Ahmed Shaheed which appeared in "*Al-Tawhid*" a respectable journal of the time. His Arabic articles began appearing in the famous "*Al-Diya*" magazine at a regular pace. *Al-Diya*'s editors were Sayyid Sulayman Nadwi and Al-Hilali, both experts of the Arabic language. His brother advised him to translate his Urdu article on Sayyid Ahmed Shaheed into Arabic and add some more historical material. Sayyid Ahmed Shahid (martyred 1831) was the great Mujahid who started jihad against the British rule, and fell martyr a thousand miles away from his ancestral village Takyaa Kalaan. Al-Hilali advised him to get it published abroad. He sent it to and was accepted for publication by Rashid Rida for his *Al-Manar* (Egypt). Read by scholars, litereates, revolutionaries and intellectuals alike, *Al-Manar* was then the world's leading Arabic religious and literary magazine. Subsequently, Rashid Rida got the article published in Egypt in the form of a short book. That was no small tribute to a lad merely sixteen years old.

Those days he was also studying English language, some science and mathematics in the hope of entering into a secular university for a graduate course. But, after a two-year application, he gave it up on a sudden, having learnt enough of the English language and known enough of the hollowness of the new disciplines. At all events, he had learnt enough English to be able to extract required material when working on his publications. From the start his mother was completely opposed to the study of the English language. In her letters she pointed out that there were already several members of the family who had distinguished themselves on that road, and that the family was in no desperate need of another trailblazer. She said if she had a hundred children, she would put them all to the study of Arabic language. Interestingly, she wrote to him that she wished to be remembered as someone who bore an offspring (and was not sterile)!

At Deoband

In 1930 he traveled once again to Lahore; this time to study Qur'an under the famous Ahmed Ali Lahori. The Lahori accepted those as his students who had already finished their *Madrasah* courses and held 'Alim or *Fadil* degrees. It was kind of an advanced course conducted in an entirely new but effective style. Students from the whole of the Indian sub-continent were attracted to the prestigious institution. Ali Miyan arrived late and so received the coaching but could not appear for the examination. He also participated in a course held on Shah Waliyullah's "*Hujjatullahi al-Baligha*" and passed the test.

In 1932 he was sent to Darul Uloom Deoband to study *Hadith* under Hussain Ahmed Madani. He stayed there for four months during which time he also studied *Fiqh*, participating in a few sessions of Anwar Shah Kashmiri (the *Sheikh al-Shuyookh* in *Hadith* studies of the time). From there he returned once again to Lahore, this time to enrol himself as a student for the Qur'anic course. At the end of the examination when the results were announced, the other students, many of whom being several years senior to Ali Miyan, (in fact, a few specialists in one or the other discipline), protested. How could the youngest of them top the list? A re-evaluation had to be ordered before Ali Miyan could receive his degree and the distinction. Thereafter he returned to Lucknow. But a short while later Ahmed Ali Lahori urged him to come back. This time he was to spend three months in seclusion in a mosque, spending time in meditation under the supervision of Ahmed Ali Lahori himself. Even reading was disallowed during those months!

Adulthood

A Teacher

Thus qualified on all fronts, with a dozen hard copy certificates, and as many impressed on his heart and soul, he was recommended for appointment as a teacher by no less than the rector, Sayyid Sulayman Nadwi, at the prestigious Darul `Ulum Nadwatul `Ulama. The recommendation accepted, he entered Nadwah as a teacher in *Tafsir*, Arabic language, and other subjects. He had just turned twenty.

Having joined Nadwah, Ali Miyan could not have found a better place for research, studies, *Da`wah*, and writing. Teaching Qur'anic *Tafsir* (commentary), he was forced to study, virtually word by word, commentaries such as "*Kashshaf*", "*Ma`alim al-Tanzil*", "*Madarik al-Tanzil*", in addition to Rashid Rida's "*Tafsir Al-Manar*", Abul Kalam Azad's Urdu commentary "*Tarjuman al-Qur'an*", those of Abdul Majid Daryabadi, and, for difficult questions, that of "Alusi." Could there be a better start for anyone who wished to take up the cause of Islam in his later years? Added to this, the presence of renowned teachers and scholars, a general environment of learning, scholarship and piety - the place was a dream come true. Later, teaching "History of the Arabic Language" gave him a sound footing in the language and taught him expressions and usage. He ended by teaching Shah Waliyy Allah's "*Hujjatullahi al-Baligha*" a philosophical work written in a fine literary style.

During those early days at Nadwah, when he also got married, Ali Miyan was chosen to represent the institute and invite Dr. Ambedkar and his community to Islam.

Dr. Ambedkar was a lower-caste Hindu leader, who had realized that so long as he and hundreds of million others like him remained Hindus, they would never be able to lead a respectful life in India and find their rightful place in the community. He announced that he was studying various religions and would be soon choosing one for adoption. Ali Miyan met him in Bombay, found a copy of the Qur'an and a few other Islamic titles on his desk and made a strong appeal for Islam. Ambedkar however, opted for Budhdhism. His conversion of course did not make any difference. Those few who converted remained low caste, while the great majority remained Hindus. The doctor hadn't perhaps realized that most of his community were resigned to their fate as those created as serfs for the upper caste. It is interesting to note, however, that when Ali Miyan was leaving for Bombay, his Arabic teacher, Sheikh Muhammad the Arab, whispered into his ears in a choking voice, that if Ambedkar asked him who would give him - a new Muslim – a daughter into marriage, he could tell him that an Arab - a descendant of the (Madinan) *Ansar* - was ready to offer his daughter!

The First Book

Year 1936 gave him the opportunity to travel to Tonk where the remnants of the descendants of Sayyid Ahmed Shahid were living, notably his great grandson Muhmmad Isma`il. There he chanced to lay hands on a work running into several volumes detailing the life, times and struggle of Sayyid Ahmed Shahid. The work inspired him and it was here, a little before sunrise, that with his feet dipped in the river Banas - at which surely Sayyid Ahmed and the Mujahideen accompanying him would have time and again performed *wudu* – Ali Miyan wrote the foreword to his first book *Seerat Sayyid Ahmed Shaheed.*

Built on the Arabic article he had earlier got published in *Al-Manaar*, he finished writing the Urdu *Seerat Sayyid Ahmed Shaheed* by the end of 1937. He had it with him when he went to Lahore to meet with Dr. Iqbal. Although the poet was sick he gave him more time than was expected of a person who was destined to die in that sickness. However, Ali Miyan, mindful of his sickness, didn't have the courage to ask him for a foreword for the book. It was decreed to be written by Sayyid Sulayman Nadwi who produced a piece of its own class for a work that was to prove a landmark for Ali Miyan. The book hoisted him up, installing him right among the rank of the leading writers of the time.

It was during those days (1938) that Mawlana Ashraf Ali Thanwi fell sick and went down to Lucknow for treatment. He stayed there for quite a while. Scholars milled around him. Ali Miyan was one of those who visited him regularly.

As if for the Divine Will to prepare him intellectually for the writing of text books for Nadwah, a task only expert educationists can perform well, in 1938 he was asked to write a book on Islam for the Islamic courses offered in the Aligarh Muslim University. With the manuscript approved, he was called to Aligarh to stay there for a month and a half and improve on it - under the guidance and supervision of experienced professors including the giant Sayyid Sulayman Ashraf. In its wake the book earned him a neat sum of Rs. 500 as prize, (being equivalent of about 50,000 today). It also earned him two congratulatory letters from Sayyid Sulayman Nadwi, a prize by itself.

The year 1939 saw the publication of *Seerat Sayyid Ahmed Shaheed*. It was not the life history of an individual. It was the history of a Jihadic struggle to establish the Islamic system of life on a patch of land. Accordingly, it was preceded by efforts to cleanse the body politic of the Muslim *Ummah* of the sub-continent of *Shirk* (Association with Allah) and *Bid'ah* (innovation in Islam). Tens of thousands were encouraged to repent, enter into an allegiance with Sayyid Ahmed Shahid, the leader of the movement whose most eloquent spokesman was Shah Ismail Shahid.

After considerable reformation, deliberations and preparations, Jihad was finally launched in the Sarhad area (1823). Its final target was the British occupation but had to start with the Sikhs who controlled the region. However, once the struggle began, the powerful Muslim landlords of the area stood up against the movement. Fighting the two forces, Sikh and Muslim, the top leaders of the movement were martyred in Balakoat, in Karbala-like fashion, and the movement died in the same fashion as that led by Imam Hussein.

At a time when the Muslims were being beaten on every front, their lands were under colonial rules, the youth were feeling humiliated and let down by their scholars and leaders who would not advise them take up arms against the established regimes, this rekindling of the Jihad memories through the life of Sayyid Ahmed Shahid, ran an electric current through the youth and the religiously committed. Some people read it ten times over. It drew appreciation even from a man of Ashraf Ali Thanwi's caliber.

Prompted by the inadequacy of classical Arabic Readers designed for senior students in the good old days, Ali Miyan took up the task of preparing a new anthology of Arabic prose and poetry. For the first time writings of such old masters as Muhiuddin Ibn al-Arabiyy (Sheikh al-Akbar), Hasan al-Busri, Mas`udi, Ghazali, Ibn Jawzi, Ibn Hibban, Ibn Taymiyyah, Ibn Qayyim, Ibn Khaldun and Shah Wali Allah were included in the work entitled *Mukhtarat* (Selections). In a couple of years the book reached the Arab lands and several institutions were quick to incorporated it among their course books. It is still used for Master Degree courses in several universities in India. In 1987 Saudi Arabian education authorities also prescribed the book for high school level courses and it underwent a reprint in Jeddah.

While teaching Arabic language at Nadwah Ali Miyan also felt that the famous six-volume Egyptian text book *Al-Qira'atu al-Rashidah* was quite inadequate, if not unfit, for the religious institutions. It has heavy secular overtones. Besides, it speaks of places and discusses topics familiar to the Egyptians alone. The sub-continent Indians hardly feel themselves related to those parts. Surely, an equivalent was the need of the day. Called *Al-Qira'at al-Raashidah* it was prepared by Ali Miyan in three volumes in about 2 years time. It won appreciation by way of inclusion in the Arabic courses in local schools. By 1944 he also brought out another set of children's books for the religious schools entitled *Stories of the Prophets for Children* - in Arabic. This one won the appreciation of even Sayyid Qutb who wrote a foreword for its second print. The book was soon included in the syllabi of various countries including Saudi Arabia. After quite a gap, Ali Miyan followed up the first three volumes with a fourth in 1975 and a fifth in 1977. The five together cover all the major Prophets mentioned in the Qur'an. A little later he followed up the children's series with *Al-Seerah al-Nabawiyyah,* (Life of the Prophet), also in Arabic, for adults. It was also well received and was included as a course material by various universities of the Arab world. Once when Ali Miyan himself visited Badr (nowadays a remote town), he found that the book was being read out to a circle of devotees in the town mosque.

Way Apart

In 1939 he met another important figure of the century, Mawlana Manzoor Ahmed No`mani. The Mawlana had read his *Seerat Sayyid Ahmed Shaheed* and had asked him through a letter if, beyond words, Ali Miyan was interested in some practical steps towards reformation and renaissance. Soon the two were on a track together, traveling to various parts of northern India in search of a movement or collective work that they could join or launch themselves. Preparation of the youth for a Jihadic struggle was one of the objectives. During those days Mawlana Mawdudi had toured through the Mewat region (now Haryana) meeting Mawlana Ilyas and studying the reformation movement that the Mawlana had launched among the masses. Much impressed, Mawlana Mawdudi wrote a powerful article on the *Tablighee* movement for his *Tarjuman al-Qur'an*. The article drew the attention of both Ali Miyan and Manzoor No`mani. It was also during that journey that for the first time he met the famous Sheikh Abdul Qadir who ran his *Khanqah* from Ra'epur. In the final leg, the journey took him to Nizamuddin, the center of *Tablighee* movement. He came back very much impressed by the effectiveness of the work, the simplicity of its founder and workers, and the depth of sincerity found in the rank and file.

The year 1940 took him closer to Mawlana Mawdudi who had launched his own *Jamat-e-Islami* movement in the year 1937. Ali Miyan and Manzoor No`mani were the natural first few of those who responded enthusiastically. Ali Miyan became its full-fledged member in 1941 and was given the charge of the Lucknow wing of the

Jama`ah. But, by 1942 there were already controversies over some of Mawlana Mawdudi's writings in which he had spoken of the scholars of Islam in a disparaging manner. There were suggestions in the Lahore meeting of the senior members of the Jama`ah that Mawlana Mawdudi should resign as the movement-leader. Ali Miyan voted for his continuance as the Amir. He felt that the step demanded would only mean some window dressing. It wouldn't change the character of the Jama`ah.

Nevertheless, he felt that there was an inordinate reverence for Mawlana Mawdudi among the Jama`ah members. Mawdudi's writings were treated as the last word on any topic and hence beyond any criticism. Not surprisingly, the members showed hardly any disposition towards the writings of other scholars, preachers or reformers, of the past or the present. For many of those who had been won over to the cause of the Jama`ah by Mawdudi's writings, and whose reading "other than that" was quite modest, if any, Mawlana Mawdudi was the very epitome of learning and a kind of genius that the Islamic world hadn't produced for a thousand years. But, more alarming was the tendency to belittle the scholars of Islam, both past and present, not too infrequently, even by the very senior members of the Jama`ah. It was to such an inordinate level that it could be regarded as the culture of the Jama`ah. Further, and more importantly, there didn't seem to be a perceptible in-depth quality change in the rank and file of the Jama`ah members, nor the realization or acknowledgment of the fact of it missing, not to speak of an urgent and pressing need to address the issue. In the common man's oft-repeated words of evaluation, the Jama'ah work was more brain and intelligence, less soul and spirit, more earthly and less heavenly; the demand on the individual being more on the outer dressing than on meaningful inner changes.

Further, to Ali Miyan, Mawlana Mawdudi's personality did not appear as charming and attractive as his writings appeared. He wrote to Mawlana Mawdudi about the struggle within, although he wouldn't have written to him how impressive the personality of Mawlana Ilyas was, and how deeply religious his entire life, to the finest detail, which stood in such noticeable contrast. But Mawlana Mawdudi did not appreciate any variant opinion within his Jama'ah, and so, as was his customary, advised him to quit. Although the membership ended then and there and coldness in the relationship, Ali Miyan did not announce the dissociation for full 35 years until he wrote in 1977 a critique on Mawdudi's *Islam ki Char Bunyadi Istalahen* (Four Basic Conceptual Terms of Islam). Ali Miyan's book was titled *'Asr-e-Hazir men Deen ki Tafheem wa Tashreeh* (Islam's Interpretation in the Modern Times) which refuted Mawdudi's ideas expressed in *Islam ki Chaar*.. He thought the ideas in the book were completely off the track and gave a new turn to the understanding of Islam, especially for those who did not have direct access to the Islamic sources. The two remained on cordial terms though: Ali Miyan never criticized him publicly or openly. But the breach in the outlook, methodology of reformation work, and the objectives that were to be laid before the eyes, remained to the end. As Ali Miyan wrote later, Mawlana Mawdudi was a brilliant critic of the Western material culture and civilization, and a forceful spokesman of the Islamic causes, but not very successful when he attempted a new interpretation of the religion of Islam, its spirit, or undertook to explain the ultimate religious truths. Mawlana Mawdudi seemed to have as much drawn from the Western thought and ideology for his own understanding of the religion of Islam as he criticized it: a doctor who fell victim to his patient's malady.

The truth is, the two scholars stood quite a bit apart and could not have gone along together for long. What was primary to one was secondary to another. One was down to earth rationalist, while the other was downright moralist and spiritualist. To Mawlana Mawdudi, the past (covering almost a thousand years) was the intellectual albatross that the *Ummah* sooner discarded, the better for it. According to him, you looked at it to find out "why" you were, and "where" you were in your decline. To Abul Hasan Ali, it was a legacy worth preserving: you looked at the past to find out "how much" you had declined. To Mawdudi, the *Ummah* needed a fresh kick-start, on a fresh trail, with a fresh agenda. Abul Hasan Ali envisaged the *Ummah*'s journey into the future as a continuation of the past, on the well-trodden path as taken by the *Salaf*, the Imams, the Mujaddidun, the renowned scholars, and, not to forget, what was anathema to Mawdudi, the *Shuyukh* and the great Sufis. Mawdudi would say, "forget the past except for the first generation or two (but that also with a grudge)." To Ali Miyan, the *Ummah* only needed a fresh resolve. To Mawdudi, it needed a fresh launch. Mawlana Mawdudi would never mention in his writings those who had left a legacy behind them, but critically. Ali Miyan spoke of them lovingly. Surely, one would have suspected the future author of *Khilafat wa Mulukiyyat* in the other, while the other would have perceived in him the future biographer of *Hazrat Nizamuddin Awliayaa*. Surely, the two scholars, although both deeply committed to the cause of Islam, stood poles apart.

Tablighee Jama`at

Nevertheless, Mawlana Mawdudi's article introducing the *Tablighee* movement was inspiring enough. Ali Miyan felt a pressing urge to meet its founder Mawlana Ilyas. The first meeting swept him off his feet. Sincerity, simplicity, sacrifice, humility, love of Allah, care of the people, accurate understanding of the religion and its demands, complete confidence that the truth would prevail, and many other qualities that one only read in books describing the first generation Muslims, were richly present in Mawlana Ilyas. In fact, these qualities reflected in some measure or the other, in all those who came under the Mawlana's influence and were serving the cause of the Tablighee movement. Ali Miyan was deeply impressed by him and his work, and was immediately won over to the cause. In fact, it was not very difficult for him to be won over. He had done a good amount of reading on reformation movements of the past, and having seen another movement outbudding, knew the difference, as he put it, between, "Two movements: one (which he had just abandoned) relied on intelligence, voracious reading, vast knowledge, and which had appeared as a reaction to certain historical factors, while, the other (which he was about to embrace) had its roots in devotion, a strong belief in Allah, an in-depth understanding of the Qur'n, a comprehension of the Prophet's life that was steeped in love, and a true and sincere adherence to Islamic principles."

Soon he began to work in earnest and established an effective Tablighee network at Lucknow. Initially, he involved the students of Nadwah, which in fact proved to be beneficial to the institution that seemed to be on the road to becoming a mere seat of learning, instead of a seat of religious revival, Da`wah and Jihad. Mawlana Ilyas, eager to draw in scholars and the scholarly to the movement, fully appreciated his contribution, and sent his guidelines continually until his death in 1944. Surely, Ali Miyan too profited from his communications and received a few lessons that served him well throughout the coming years of *Da`wah* works.

After the initiation of the work in Lucknow, Ali Miyan moved on to work in surrounding cities and provinces. By 1942 the work had expanded so much that he resigned from the teaching post at Nadwah to devote his full time and attention to the Tablighee work. Nevertheless, pressed up by financial needs, in a year's time he was back as a teacher. But by 1945 he had said a final good-bye to paid jobs, depending there onward, on whatever he earned from his writings, which of course didn't amount to much. Several big offers that came his way from universities, both Indian and foreign, and several lean patches during which he and his family were on the verge of starvation, wouldn't alter his resolve.

Meanwhile, with the expansion of the Tablighee work, he felt that an expansion in the agenda of the reformation movement was necessary. Although the new Amir, Mawlana Yusuf, Mawlana Ilyas' son, was not well disposed to any such expansion of the agenda, on his own Ali Miyan introduced a few changes in his personal approach. The Qur'anic and *Dars al-Hadith* sessions held by him, Mawlana Manzoor Ahmed No'mani, and others in the Lucknow Tablighee headquarters were steps in that direction.

Between 1945 and 1947 he toured the northern Indian region several times over: from the East to the West, in his efforts to popularize the work. In June 1947 it was decided that he should tour the Hejaz area (Saudi Arabia) along with a few others and popularize the movement among the Arabs. He traveled with his wife and mother and spent almost a whole year there. In Hejaz he was able to win over quite a few intellectuals and *Shuyukh* to the Tablighee cause. There were many doubts and lots of skepticism about the method and efficacy of the work. (Strangely, the initial skepticism has a history of persistence). His friendship with Sheikh 'Umar b. al-Hasan Aal al-Sheikh, one of the descendants of Sheikh Abdul Wahhab, and the chief of the Higher Body of scholars in Saudi Arabia helped him in moving the movement. The Sheikh was so convinced that on various occasions he spoke openly in favor of the movement without which perhaps no work could ever have been done there.

Maa Dha ..

Ali Miyan, had however, been thinking on the situation the *Ummah* was passing through, about what were the causes of its decline, and what impact its decline had on the world. In 1944 he began to write the book that did for him what *Seerat Sayyid Ahmed Shahid* had done for him in the Indian sub-continent: introducing him to the Arab and Islamic world as someone whose next title could be awaited. Completed in 1948, the book was written with a pen that was markedly different from those of the modernists as well as the classical. It expressed thoughts that were neither eastern nor western, a theme that was innovative, an approach that was novel, a style that was fresh, ideas that were exciting, a language that was classical, and a conclusion that was refreshing for the tired souls. (Imam Hasan al-Banna' had just been assassinated and Ikhwan was undergoing a ban in Egypt). After *Fi Zilal al-Qur'an* and *Ma`alim fi 'l-Tareeq* of Sayyid Qutb, no other book gained as much popularity in the Arab world as this one: *Ma Dha Khasira `Alam bin-hitat al-Muslimin* ("What did the world lose from Muslim Decline," - but the Engllish version is known as "Islam and the World"). Nor has any other work exercised such extensive influence. Although first printed in 1951, even at the end of the century it was enough in the Arab world to introduce Ali Miyan as the author of Maa Dhaa.." It is estimated that the book has undergone, to this date, over a hundred reprints.

Once Ali Miyan asked one of his students if he had read it. When told he hadn't, he spontaneously remarked, "In the Arab world a man is not considered educated if he hasn't read this book." Later he began to wonder if he had spoken the truth. But when he met Yusuf al-Qaradawi he told him, "When we were students in Egypt, we used to hear that someone who had not read this book was not an educated person." It is reported that one of the professors at Cambridge, an Orientalist remarked, "If there was a law in Britain allowing for banning a book, I would recommend that this book be banned entry. This book strikes at the Western civilization, like a bolt of lightening." And, in the words of an eastern writer, the book changed the Muslim position from defense to that of offense.

At its start, the book details out the situation of the world pervious to the advent of Islam: the Roman, Persian, Chinese and Indian worlds, showing that the world was then sunk in injustice, misery, moral bankruptcy and debauchery. It also illustrates the situation in the Arab world and, specifically, in the Arabian Peninsula. Ali Miyan shows that it was, (as evidenced by the judgement of the contemporaries, in the unanimous voice of both Arabs as well as non-Arabs), not at the bottom of the world in injustice, moral bankruptcy and debauchery, but right in a pit of its own. It was a pit which, if visited by those who were at the bottom of the non-Arab world, would leave them gasping.

Next it moved to showing what changes the personality and teachings of Prophet Muhammad (on whom be peace) brought into the lives of the earliest converts, also showing what it was that could be counted as the distinguishing and outstanding part of the Prophetic message. What were the objectives and the means that were adopted to attain those objectives? He also showed what the central theme of the Prophetic message was, which had to be kept before the eyes by every reformation movement. The third chapter considers the rise and fall of the Turkish Caliphate, discussing the reasons that led to the great decline. That is followed by the most important part of the book which discusses the reasons of the rise of the Western power and leadership, and why it was that the West abandoned Christianity and took on materialism as its goal of life and civilization. The chapter also points out the dangers the world faces, real and perceptible - time would confirm - as a result of the change in leadership, from Islamic, (a combination of intellectual, moral and spiritual), to the Western (a combination of mental, physical and animalistic prowess) that accepted no moral binding, saw no spiritual upturning and believed in no other objective but the ever more exploitation of man and materials. Islam on the other hand being what it is: an "optimum-best package," allowed for the building of the body and re-construction of the world, but, at the same time, delivered enough sugar-burner to the body to assure good health. Further, in contrast to the Western system, which allowed no reprieve, Islam made enough space in what was already built to allow for ever more numbers of those who labored to sneak a siesta in, before the next construction activity began. Such an Islam - the companion-runner that halted the runner before he dropped dead out of exhaustion - the world had no choice but to accept, willy-nilly, and the Muslims too had no choice but to live by. That is because, if the Muslims fell for something else, or something else was targeted at them, in either case they would be the losers. Muslims are like water melons. If the knife fell on the water melon, it would cut it, and if the water melon fell on the knife, it would be cut. In either case, Muslims would be the ones to suffer a cut.

That reminder is followed by suggestions as to how the Islamic world can regain its true position: not as leaders, but as demonstrative co-workers, and save the world and themselves from the impending gradual, but sure destruction. Faith and action, spirit and intellect, morals and ideals, industries and military, were to be the tools that the Muslims were to skillfully employ. The Arabs were invited to play the leadership role, reminding them that they were no more weightier than scrap material of the human order if they did not realize, acknowledge and follow the precepts of the Prophet raised among them.

Written partly in India, partly in the Arab world, the book was not exactly a hot cake at the start, but it remained throughtout the following half a century its sale records kept rising. It underwent dozens of reprints and was translated into major Islamic languages and the second Arabic print was decorated with Sayyid Qutb's powerful foreword who was himself much moved by the work. In 1982 Dar al-Qalam (Kuwait) published 100,000 copies, of which 92,000 went to the Saudi Arabian Ministry of Education. Once Sheikh 'Abdullah 'Abdul Ghani Khayyat, the Imam al-Haram, read out a long passage from this book in his Friday sermon. Ali Miyan thanked him when he met him later. The Imam replied that he had been quoting from it quite regularly.

To the Elite

In addition to *Ma Dha* ..., another article that he wrote before taking up the journey helped in introducing him to the Arab religious and literary circles. Entitled, *"To the Elite of the Islamic World,"* it was originally written for the representatives of the Islamic countries that were attending a conference at Delhi called by Nehru. The paper couldn't be presented in the conference and so was later published in the newspaper *Dawn*. It was a powerful article which pointed out that the Muslim *Ummah* came into existence at a time when the world was not short of skilled and specialized men who could build and beautify the earth. Artists, architects, planners, builders, artisans, administrators and statesmen were aplenty at that time. The need at that time was for a new nation that had its roots in right kind of beliefs and ideals: those that the humanity lacked. The clashes that took place at Makkah and Madinah, between the early Muslims and pagans occurred precisely because the Muslims stood for beliefs, principles and values.

Early in Islam, when the Quraysh made an offer to the Prophet to accept their leadership, wealth and women, in return of cessation of his Prophetic activities, and when the Prophet decline, preferring to fight it out at Badr, Uhad and Hunayn, (undergoing severe hardships and exposing himself and the movement to great dangers), then, it was to demonstrate that it was not power, wealth, or any other worldly objective that the Muslims had before them. The pagans received the message in no ambiguous terms that the Muslims were fighting for faith, morals and principles. But the situation with the Muslim peoples is very different in the contemporary world.

They seem to have accepted the same principles of life that the Prophet and the Companions fought against. If there happens to be an international conference today, in which Muslim nations are also represented, along with the world community, the Muslims would be unrecognizable and indistinguishable from the rest of the participants. Neither in words nor in appearance, nor in actions and activities, would they be any different from those others in the gathering who hold dear the same beliefs and ideals as the pagan Quraysh did. If those of the Quraysh slaughtered at Badr were brought back to life and if they asked the Muslims of today, "How can you justify your present attitude towards those principles and morals over which you slaughtered us?" - then, how will they reply?

It was another of those powerful themes that Ali Miyan was to use repeatedly when addressing the Arabs during the time he spent in Hejaz and other parts of the Arab world between 1947 and 1951.
He wrote another powerful article those days, this one in Urdu. It was not universally appreciated though. It was too frank not to hurt a people that wore a "holier than thou" attitude. It criticized the Muslims over their outlook towards this life, and their attitudes towards the challenges they were facing. He placed his diagnostic finger on the national weaknesses that seemed to be eating away at the root of the body politic of the *Ummah*, and were about to acquire the

status of their national character. The weaknesses that he pointed out were:

(a) Tendency to accord preference to personal interests over those of the nation at the cost of principles.
(b) Refusal to accept the challenge the West had thrown at them.
(c) Refusal to plunge into action and put up work hard.
(d) Show of cowardice.
(e) Blind following of the secular and national leadership, and
(f) Excessive outpouring of emotions and sentiments in writings and speeches.

He pointed out that the depth of intellectual and moral decline of the Muslims had reached such proportions that they seemed to gloat over the calamities of their enemies and almost waited for them to occur. Their moral bankruptcy had suffered such decline that they were not ready to concede that their adversaries had anything good in them. Because of their inaction, they seemed to become so dispirited that they had lost self-confidence, imagined themselves weaker than they were, and over-estimated the strength and capabilities of their adversaries. The reason for such decline seemed to him to be the result of modern education that the colonial powers had designed for them.

A Charged Atmosphere

Having laid the foundation for Tablighee work in the Hejaz, Ali Miyan returned in 1948 to a sub-continent that had undergone division. And, the day he landed at Lucknow, Gandhi was assassinated. Probably it is from that shock that he took up the peace call that dominated his later life among his countrymen throughout the rest of the century.

By 1948 Ali Miyan had returned to an India where tremendous transformations had taken place within a short period of time since independence. Hindus had turned highly prejudiced, offensive and violent. People in high places who were supposed to talk sense, were uttering non-sense. Important figures such as, Purshottam Das Tandum, Sampurnandji, and others were in the forefront asking Muslims why they couldn't give their children Hindu names? Why they couldn't write Urdu in Hindi script? Why did they break their fasts with dates? Why did they cling to their culture? And so on.

Muslims were too overwhelmed, too fearful and too diffident to answer. Many of their prominent leaders had left for Pakistan and blamed the Muslims themselves for the situation. Muslims felt lost, unable to cope with the situation. It was only Mawlana Hifzur Rahman Sew-harwi (the writer of "Life-histories of the Prophets") who spoke out openly and fearlessly against the attacks reminding the Hindus that having opposed partition of the country, what he and his organization (Jami`at Ulamaa-e-Hind) were paying as price, was something the Hindus criticizing them had never paid.

`Ali Miyan called for a conference of scholars, intellectuals, leaders and social workers in which he read out a speech inviting the participants to gather their strength, look forward positively, and build up anew. Could a religion be defeated, which had followers who said, like Abu Bakr did, "Will this religion suffer damage while I am alive?" Could such a religion ever face threat of extinction?

In 1950 he was back in Hejaz. The upward journey was done in the company of Sheikh Abdul Qadir Ra'epuri. Apart from Hajj, the idea was to work for the Tablighee cause. Other important Tablighee workers were already in. At arrival by sea he found a sea of change between the Arabia of 1947 and that of 1950. The new generation had swiftly opted for Westernism. With the United States as the new *Qiblah*, materialistic way of life seemed to have taken a strong hold equally of the commoner as well as the elite, the literate as well as the illiterate. He realized immediately that in comparison to the Western storm, the *da'wah* efforts, books and pamphlets were mere ripples in the sea.

The first introductory session proved to be a test session rather than a speech session. The selected audience consisted of a member of the Saudi Consultative Council, a few editors of influential magazines, officers from various ministries and a couple of highly placed people.

With their usual craft the Arabs dug into him. Satisfied that after all he knew sufficient Arabic, was familiar with writers like Taha Hussain, 'Aqqad etc., knew all about communism and could manage some English, they arranged that he should speak on the radio. Several "Radio Speeches" helped him in reaching a wide audience. However, soon he realized that Egypt was the literary and cultural capital of the Arab world. Cultural ethos, literary zenre, ideas and ideologies were imported from across the Nile. If he wished to exercise any influence on the youth of this part of the world, he thought he will have to first address those of the Egypt.

In Egypt

With the travel expenses jointly arranged by his brother and *Sheikh al-Hadith* (Mawlana Zakariyyah), he traveled to Egypt. Cairo then (1951) was a galaxy of scholars, literary masters and *Shuyukh*. Some of those living in Cairo at that time were greatest figures of the Islamic world: Dr. Ahmed Amin Bek, Taha Hussain, `Abbas Mahmud al-`Aqqad, Muhammad Husain al-Haykal, Tawfiq al-Hakim, Ahmed Hasan Zayyat, Mansur Fahim Pasha, Sheikh Abdul Majeed Saleem (Sheikh al-Azhar), Hasanayn Muhammad Makhluf, Ahmad b. `Abdur Rahman (Hasan al-Banna's father), Hamid al-Fiqi, Abdul Wahhab bek Khallaf, Zahid al-Kawthari, Fu'ad Abdul Baqi, Mufti Sayyid al-Hussaini, Abdul Karim Rayfi, Abdul Rahman `Azzam Pasha, Amin Mahmud Khattab, Muhiudding Khateeb, Sayyid Qutb, Mahmud Muhammad Shakir, Muhammad al-Ghazali, Sa`id Ramadan and many others. `Ali Miyan and his colleagues were all but lost, invisible in the galaxy. " *Ma Dha* ..." and Egyptian youths came to his rescue.

They took him around to young men's associations, hostels, seminars and weekly meetings, allowing him the opportunity to address young men from Egypt, Turkey, Syria, Indonesia, Eriteria and other parts of the Islamic world. Members of the Ikhwan (then undergoing ban) took him around to almost an end to end tour of Egypt. As he moved along, so did the Tablighee workers who worked among the masses. While `Ali Miyan's platform was public halls, they operated through the mosques. It was during those tours that he realized the depth of Ikhwan influence, not merely in big cities, but small towns and even villages. Sheikh Hasan al-Banna' (who had been martyred a little earlier) seemed to have left his influence on every facet of Egyptian life and every section of the society. He was not only moved by the wide expanse of the work, but also the depth of reformation among the individuals.

Sincerity, love of Islam, high discipline, sacrifice, brotherhood, moral rectitude, hard work, realism, interest in constructive social works, undaunted faith in Islam – these were qualities visible in every individual who came under the influence of Ikhwan. All kinds of men: young and old, the laity and the scholar, rich and poor bore qualities that, according to `Ali Miyan, he never happened to have seen earlier or would ever see later in any section of people anywhere else. From Egypt he went to Sudan, then to Syria, Jordan, Palestine, taking the Tablighee work with him, although himself delivering lectures to the educated class. Touching Hejaz again, he was back in India after a tour that stretched over a period of 13-14 months

Change of Heart?

Back in India now, an important change in his approach was brought by the observation that was needed to address the non-Muslims of this country along with Muslims. "Peace first" was the idea that came to his mind again and again. Addressing huge mixed gatherings - Muslim and non-Muslim, initially from the Tablighee platforms - he pointed out that the primary reasons for the modern degradation were an insatiable love of this world, selfishness, and weakening of moral values. Mawlana Manoor No`mani was once again with him in several tours that were undertaken for this purpose. They toured together the north-Indian regions.

The non-Muslims generally received the messages well, but, although by 1957 it could develop into a full fledged movement if given an organizational structure, it did not bear much fruit since it did not have any written program, a party manifesto or plan of action. The demand was restoration of good sense and moralistic behavior: not very attractive themes for the modern Industrial societies.

Nonetheless, Ali Miyan was convinced that in the changing conditions, methods of invitation and propagation needed to be improved and new vistas must be opened. If movements do not move with time, did not answer the new challenges, did not find solutions to new problems, they'd get frozen. Human society would benefit less and less from their frozen state. He had these ideas in mind even during the time of Mawlana Ilyas, but perhaps, Mawlana's personality was too powerful for any suggestion of change in style, content or approach. He spoke of the need to the new leaders including the *Ameer* Mawlana Yusuf.

The issue was discussed during several consultative meetings, but he found little inclination towards any change in methods, revision or inclusion of new agenda. On the other hand the Tablighee movement was still doing some good work, which, as always, was better than nothing. Indeed, from a certain angle, the results were satisfactory, and, therefore, there seemed to be no wisdom in pressing on the changes. But, that didn't mean the need was not there, and that those who could do better ought to follow the footsteps of those who, without their personal knowledge and experience, were bound to keep close to the line drawn for them by others.

Ali Miyan was convinced however that a change was essential. And so, if others who acknowledged that something was lacking, but did not know how to go about filling the gap, then, Ali Miyan would do it on his own. Therefore, the work at Lucknow, in which he and Mawlana Manzoor No`mani played the leading roles, began to adopt two approaches side by side. The standard approach was for the masses, and the special for the educated. The work among the Arabs that he was asked to introduce and popularize, also needed a new methodology. With their direct contacts with the Qur'an and *Sunnah*, the Arab audience was certainly different form the non-Arabic audience. Ali Miyan had to adopt new techniques. His wider exposure to various problems that the Muslim *Ummah* faced in various parts of the world, problems which could not be solved with a single formula led him to work for change in methods. Further, his own readings of the past and present reformation movements, in different parts of the world, was another factor that had its slow but certain effect, and led him more and more away from the standard Tablighee approach.

In 1969, by which time Ali Miyan had also got involved in various other social and community activities in India, he had to shift his residence away from the Tablighee center in Lucknow. He had lived there for almost 15 years – monk like - in order to be available at call. Now he shifted to the Guest Quarters in Nadwah. Mawlana Manzoor No`mani, another pillar of Tabligh at Lucknow, who had lived in the same street as the Lucknow Tablighee center, also moved out to another part of the city. The two took away with them their special style of work and left the standard bearers to do the standard work. Not that the romance was over or that there were serious differences. But, the old stalwarts were simply not available at call, as before. Yest, the change in residence was symbolic.

Saviors of Islamic Spirit

Despite his deep involvement in *Da`wah* works, Ali Miyan hadn't laid aside his pen. In 1953 he began to write a new book, " *Tarikh-e-Da`wat wa `Azimat*" (*Saviors of Islamic Spirit*). Its first volume came out in 1954. It consisted of life histories and achievements of Islamic renowned personalities between `Umar ibn `Abd al-`Aziz of the first century and Mawlana Jalaluddin Rumi of the seventh century.

Mawlana Ra'epuri read it several times over. Even Manazir Ahsan Geelani had generous words of praise for it. Its second volume came out in 1956. It presented the life of Imam Ibn Taymiyyah and his students. The third was written between 1961 and 1963 when he was suffering from cataract in the eye and had to dictate his writings. It consists of the lives of Sheikh Nizamuddin Awliya' and Sheikh Sharfuddin Yahya Minyari. The fourth part, that speaks of Mujaddid Alf-Thani came out as late as 1980. The intention was to follow up with a fifth volume on Shah Waliy Allah and his students, but it never came to be written.

In 1955 Dr. Mustafa Rifa'i, who was a professor of Law at the University of Damascus and a member of Jordanian parliament, invited him to join the staff at the newly opened College of Shari'ah in the University. He declined, but agreed to go as a visiting professor. The lectures delivered at intervals, over a three month period, were well attended by scholars, intellectuals and the religiously committed. He also spoke on the Radio twice. In some of the speeches he criticized the Arabs for their present role and their un-Islamic attitudes, which manifested itself in the powerful Arab nationalism. On one occasion he told them that he didn't expect that the Arabs would deliver the message of Islam to non-Arabs and then abandon it themselves.

From Syria he traveled to Lebanon and then to Turkey delivering lectures. In June 1956 he was back in Syria to attend an Islamic conference in which were also present Mawlana Shafi' Deobandi,

Mawlana Mawdudi and Mawlana Zafar Ahmed Ansari, some of the notable figures of the sub-continent. He was made a member of the prestigious "Literary Society" of Damascus.

Back in India, he strengthened his ties with the remaining *Shuyukh* of the dwindling orders. Sheikh Shah Muhammad Ya`qub, Mawlana Wasiullah, Haji `Abdul Ghafoor, Mawlana Warith Hasan and Mawlana Abdus Shakoor Farooqui were the tail-enders of the caravan that had packed and gone. At Nadwah he took up some new subjects for teaching, including Sahih Bukhari. In 1958 he brought out another work of importance. It was about the Qadiyani movement. He was visiting Sheikh Abdul Qadir Ra'epuri in Pakistan. The Sheikh complained to him that the Qadiyani movement was getting stronger there and wished that Ali Miyan could write a book on the menace. Ali Miyan was without the usual reference works, but the Sheikh insisted that he begin writing then and there. Finally, Ali Miyan agreed and produced a work in Arabic, that was printed and published in the Arab world in hundreds of thousands. It was later translated into Urdu. Its English version was done by Dr. Zafar Ishaq Ansari (translator of *Tafheem al-Qur'an*, and son of the energetic Zafar Ahmed Ansari of Pakistan). Written entirely in an objective manner, consisting of arguments that do not provoke anger, the book has become a kind of standard text on Qadiyanism and deserves to be included as course book in the universities.

The New Apostasy

In 1958 when Sa'id Ramadan had to travel to Germany for his doctorate degree, he asked 'Ali Miyan to take over the editorship of his magazine "*Al-Muslimoon*" that he brought out from Dasmascus. Two editorials that he wrote for that magazine were combined into one called, "*An Apostasy that has no Abu Bakr to Combat*" and published separately as a booklet." He pointed out therein the dangers of a new kind of *apostasy* that had appeared in the wake of Western cultural onslaught on the world of Islam. It was coming in through the channels of modern education. It was the most massive ever *apostasy* movement since the time of the Prophet (*saws*). As against previous waves of *apostasy* minor in nature, this one had a different character. Those who had apostatized under its influence did not deny God, and did not go to a Church, Temple or elsewhere to announce the change of persuasion. Nor does the Islamic society take any notice of someone who evinces the signs of this new kind of *apostasy*.

No Muslim ever boycotts him and no one ever sees any difference between this new apostate and a true Muslim. A large number of the educated class had already caught the disease, and seemed to be beyond cure. But the coming generations had to be saved. He pointed out the dangers of neglecting this stealthily but fast-advancing malady which would eat away at Muslim *Ummah*'s root and branch from within like termites eat away at wood. What was required was a firm resolve to fight it out with the help of a new educational system, new literature and, most of all, a new resolve.

When printed as a pamphlet it proved to be an instant hit. It sold better than hotcakes. Many organizations and institutions re-printed and published it widely. Translated into several languages, it was distributed among the pilgrims in Arafat and Mina during the Hajj season. None of his books or articles received as wide a publicity as this one did. When he was introduced to Imam Khumeini in one of the conferences of the World Assembly of Muslims at Makkah, Khomeini quipped, "Ah yes. You are the author of "*An Apostasy that* ..." I have read your article. It should have been rather entitled `*An Apostasy that has no Abul Hasan to Combat.*'" By Abul Hasan he meant Hasan's father, `Ali ibn Abi Talib!

Whatever others did to fight against the new *apostasy*, Ali Miyan himself opened a new Academy in 1959 that was to prepare and publish literature that would appeal to the new generation educated on Western lines. It was called "Academy of Islamic Research & Publication." Over a period of 25 years, it published some 200 titles in various languages and exported books to several Islamic countries.

Nadwah's Rector

In 1961 when his brother died, Ali Miyan was asked to take over the rectorship of Nadwah. Its financial problems forced him to travel to Kuwait. He had set the condition that he would only engage himself in *Da`wah* activities. Making appeals and collecting funds would be done in separate sessions by the accompanying team. He delivered speeches in mosques, academies and association halls, cautioning the Arabs over proper use of the new wealth. He also wrote a letter to

Sheikh Abdullah Salem al-Sabah - the ruler of Kuwait - pointing out the responsibility that Kuwait bore and the things it had to do to enter into the family of nations as an equal contributor. It could only do that if it pursued an Islamic agenda. He also pointed out the dangers in allowing the establishment of places of worship devoted to other religions which went against the Prophet's command that two religions ought not to exist in the Arab Peninsula.

In 1961 when the Jami`a Islamiyyah (The International Islamic University) was established in Madinah, he was offered a teaching post. In keeping with his vow not to accept a paid job, he declined. He was made a member of the consultative council of the University and traveled quite often to attend its meetings. The same year the "World Muslim League" came into being and he was also made a founding member of the organization based at Makkah. In 1962 he delivered eight lectures at the University in Madinah on the topic of "Prophethood and Prophets in the Light of the Qur'an."

The lectures were well attended. The rector Sheikh Abdul Aziz b. Abdullah b. Baaz personally sat through all the lectures. In 1963 he met Faisal b. `Abdul `Aziz who was then the Crown Prince and expressed his fears that the development pressures could completely change the Islamic character of the two holy cities Makkah and Madinah. Thereafter, when Faisal had become the King of the country, he wrote him two letters pointing out that true development did not consist merely in the availability of the means of comfort. The very class of people who make the most of the facilities made available to them - the rich and the well-to-do - have always proved in the past as an ungrateful class that rebelled against the established political system and brought revolutionary changes. It was rather the religious class which was the backbone of any country which could be relied upon for patriotism and faithfulness to it. Somewhere in 1965, he personally met the King and expressed his concern over the country's emphasis on material development. The King assured him that attention was also being paid to the heritage of the past. Ali Miyan felt however that the King was facing constraints.

Invited by Dr. Sa`id Ramadan in 1963 to attend the yearly conference of the Geneva Islamic center, he traveled there, and there on to other parts of Europe and Britain. His most important speech was "*Between East and West*" which was delivered at the London University. It was impromptu translated by Dr. Zafar Ishaq Ansari. Muhammad Asad, Dr. Hameeduallh, Dr. Zaki Ali, Dr. Abdullah Abbas Nadwi were some others present on that occasion.

Riots at Home

In the meanwhile, hatred against Muslims in India was mounting. Riots were the order of the day. But 1963 and 1964 would be remembered as the cruelest of times for Muslims. A series of riots broke out, one after another, in a chain that it was difficult to deny they were pre-planned by those who had been spreading hatred since several decades and preparing the common people for the onslaught.

Calcutta, Jamshedpur, Rourkela, and Ranchi witnessed such riots that forced a man like Jaya Prakash Narayan to say in the Parliament, "There were no limits in barbarism that were not crossed. Such horrible things were done that are impossible to imagine." Ali Miyan could no more talk of peace, responsibility, good sense and so forth. Blood patches on the walls, and skulls in the fields lying like watermelons were calling for some action.

He, Manzoor No`mani and others decided to see Vinoba Bhave, the famous social worker. The memorandum that was presented said, "India stands at a new crossroad. Should it take the road to self-destruction or to national reconstruction? The country is at a such a juncture that if a few courageous people stood up with resolve, they could change the direction. A firm word from such a person could do what governments cannot achieve. It can only be those who have the past record of honesty, integrity, patriotism, and sincerity attached to their name. According to the delegates who had the backing of Jaya Prakash Narayan, Vinoba Bhave was the man." But, disappointingly, Vinoba Bhave showed no concern for the massive human losses. He seemed to be more concerned about cows. He was fight hard to win better treatment for cows.

Disappointment with the majority community forced the Muslims to turn inward and work out other ways of achieving safety of life and property. A political platform was necessary. The need gave birth to "*Muslim Majlis-e-Mushawarat*" (The Muslim Consultative Body) of whose advisory board he became a member. It was decided that an awareness program should be launched and the sensible elements of the non-Muslim society should also be involved. A series of mass meetings were organized.

When the delegates of the *Majlis* traveled around, evoking peace, Ali Miyan spoke at Jamshedpur to a mixed audience of Hindus, Muslims and Christians, in a mass meeting chaired by the Hindu General Manager of the TATA Company. With reference to the steel industry of the TATA's, he said in his speech that "If steel was given voice it would say that I have not been created so that man may cut man's throat. If that happens then it is not I, the steel, that needs to be blamed. The blame is on those educated people who use me not for constructive but for destructive purposes." The TATA General Manager whispered in Ali Miyan's ears that there was need for more speeches of that sort.

In 1966 he penned down another important work "*The Four Pillars of Islam.*" Like many others, he had begun to be alarmed by the influential modernistic writers who were giving the rituals of Islam materialistic and utilitarian coloring. Prayers and fasts, for instance, were for self-discipline. Zakah, a solution to economic problems. Hajj, according to them was an international Conference. Ali Miyan dug out material from Imam Ghazali, Shah Waliyullah, Ibn al-Qayyim and others, strengthened with *Hadith* material and demonstrated the moral and spiritual benefits of these Islamic rituals. In a way this happens to be the most important of his writings. Admittedly, no such work exists even in the Arabic language, and perhaps will be preserved better than even *"Ma Dha.."* One wishes that his intention to write a separate book on faith and beliefs, the first pillar of Islam, had been accomplished.

Two years later in 1965 he added another important work to the list of his writings. It was originally written in Arabic, and was a kind of a sequel to " *Ma Dha* ..." It was later translated into English, entitled "*The Struggle Between Muslims and Western Ideologies.*" It analyzed the situation prevalent in every major Islamic country. The problem these Muslims were now facing was, how to treat the onslaught of the Western ways of life, culture and thought. Instead of the Muslim (political) leadership working out a compromise solution, since, total rejection was not workable, nor total acceptance advisable, they seemed to be engaged in an internal struggle.

On the one side were the political leaders and rulers who had accepted West's superiority in everything and were its staunchest protagonists in their own countries. They believed that the only path to development and progress was the Western path. They thought Islam and Islamists stand on the path of development as highway robbers, and the Islamic culture was the barrier that needed to be removed from the path. On the other side were the masses who still clung to their religion and to whom nothing made as strong an appeal as Qur'anic call. Nothing quickens their imagination better than the examples from the life of their Prophet. Unfortunately, the ruling class considers the more seriously committed individuals from among the masses as those who pose a strong challenge to its authority, and therefore spends its best energies in fighting and curbing them, creating an atmosphere of fear. Rather than this internal confrontation, or, confrontation with the West and its influence, a wiser course would be to work out ways by which the best of the Western thought and culture that did not clash with the Islamic principles be worked out and adopted. Obviously, it required courage, wisdom, hard work, and therefore, a new kind of leadership, if not a new leadership altogether. This book was also well received and was soon translated into several languages. In fact, coming out in 1968, it happened to be the last of his great works. He wrote several more afterwards, but none carried any new idea, expression or thought - at least not of the quality the earlier writings had. Incidentally, the book could only have evoked suspicion of the ruling classes, as it suggested a new kind of leadership. So, after all, they were not wrong in assuming who their true enemies were!

The 1967 Debacle

By 1968 Ali Miyan began to travel to the Arab world with quite regularity. When asked to comment on the 1967 Arab defeat and the loss of Jerusalem, in an interview conducted by the "*Al-Nadwah*" paper of Saudi Arabia, he replied, "For me the defeat, although disappointing, was not at all surprising. Many of those who draw inspiration from the Qur'an and the Sunnah were expecting this to happen. It did not require one to be prophetic to come to such a conclusion. The writings were on the wall. The Arab power was like a balloon in the air. You didn't need to predict what would happen to it if someone punctured it with a pin. The preparation for the conflict by the Arabs consisted of emotional speeches, beautiful print-media articles, thunderous radio and television talks.

These were their main weapons against Israel. If there was any unity of purpose or action, it was against their own masses. The Arab leaders were not, as the Qur'an said, *'Soft on believers and tough on unbelievers.'* They were 'soft on unbelievers and tough on believers.' Their preparation for the war was as dramatically portrayed to the public as that of the legendary Ali Baba and forty thieves. But when they actually faced the enemy, the dramatists and actors ran for their lives. The battle was real. The drama failed." When asked to comment on the reaction of the Arab masses to the disastrous defeat, he replied that it was quite disappointing.

They behaved as if nothing had happened - neither anything holy was lost, nor was there any further danger facing them. They were back to making the best of their time completely oblivious of the loss of standing among the nations of the world. In that interview he invited the rulers, leaders, journalists and those who worked out the system of education, to jointly play their constructive roles in bringing up a new generation that had some self-respect, self-confidence, and was conscious of the great legacy of Islam. If the Islamic wealth is lost, he cautioned, it will be hard to bring it back alive. In fact, this was the only thing that the Arabs could export to the rest of the world and win respect thereby.

To counter the spread of pessimism and despair he wrote an article for the Arabs giving them the glad tidings of the final victory, because they were Muslims and Arabs. He pointed out that the future didn't belong to the Jews, even if they came to occupy half of the world, because they had nothing to offer to the world. Allah's law is reflected in the verse (13: 17), "*As for the foam it passes away as scum.*" God is the Lord of the world, and not of the Israelites. He wishes to see justice, equality and respect for human rights to prevail, and not the hegemony of this or that nation or race over others. The Arabs could establish all this, because they inherited these values through the revelation that they possessed. If the Arabs rose up with a call based on these beliefs and issues, there was no reason to doubt that the future belonged to them. Little surprise that the powerful Palestinian figure, Mufti Amin al-Hussaini got the article reprinted and distributed under a new title, "*The Ultimate (victory) is for the Godfearing.*"

In 1973 he was chosen to lead a delegation of the "World Muslim League" based in Makkah to tour six Islamic countries. Afghanistan was already in turmoil then, but still there was no problem in visiting places and addressing the people. In Iran, just ten years away from the massive Shi`ite revolution, the delegation could not even smell of the on-coming typhoon that swept away the monarchic system and brought the clergy to power. Either the signs were invisible or the visiting delegates were carefully kept away from observation. He raised a question: Why a land which had produced geniuses and great minds in every field of human activity, had, since a few hundred years, been unable to produce a single great man worthy of mention. Was it because of the Shi`ite hold on the minds of its adherents that did not allow them the freedom to think, or were there other causes? This question did not bring out a satisfactory answer from the Shi`i scholars that he met there.

In Syria, it wasn't the third day of their stay in the country when the famous "*Mabahith*" (Secret Service) officers arrived at the hotel they were lodged, at their favorite time of operation: midnight, loaded them onto a car and unloaded them on the Lebanon Border. In Iraq, they were treated a little better. The delegates were allowed to offer their Friday Prayers in a mosque 10 km. off Baghdad, of course in the company of the "*Mabahith.*" In addition there were other governmental agency people who were at hand to prevent any contact between the delegate members and the common people in that deserted area. The delegates who returned to Makkah could not have had much to report on the Islamic countries of their visit. It was a triumph that they had entered those places at all.

In 1976 he had to attend the annual conference of the "Islamic Universities Federation" held that year in Morocco. In one meeting with King Hassan, who had newly ascended the throne, he expressed hope that he (Hassan) could prove to be the man the nation of Islam was hoping would appear and take its rattled ship through the rough waters, and oar it across to the shores of power, renaissance and glory. The next year he was invited to attend a conference of the MSA in the

United States. It was also an opportunity to get the cataract on the eye removed which had rendered him half blind for the last 13-14 years, unable to read out his own speeches or pen down his works. The operation was performed by a Christian doctor who became sort of friendly and didn't charge him for the operation. The next year he visited Pakistan, now under Ziaul Huq, to attend the yearly "World Muslim League" conference being held there.

Uniform Civil Code

Back home, when the government of India seriously began to consider formation of a "Uniform Civil Code" in the 70s, and, during the same year intended to take over the running of the Muslim University Aligarh, then, once again he stood up against the moves along with the Muslim scholars and intellectuals. He reminded his country-men that an educational institution was not a sugar mill from which only one kind of product was expected to roll out. That would happen if the government took over the educational institutes. Variety, and hence richness, would be the cost that would be paid for uniformity. If in any country, the government took over the educational institutions, tutoring one doctrine, producing one model of men, faithful to one political party, and the teachers and administrators reduced to executing the policies of the government, instead of vying to improve the educational standards, then, surely, nothing else would be required to destroy that country's educational system and the country itself.

When Indira Gandhi's election was declared null and void in 1975, she responded by declaring a state of Emergency in India. The special powers that the Emergency afforded were used more by her son than herself. And, the Muslims became the targets of his energies and newly acquired power. Tens of thousands of homes were demolished in the clean up drive launched by him. According to Kuldip Nayar, in Lucknow alone 10,000 homes were demolished and the inhabitants sent into the cold as shelterless refugees without a refugee status. And, when the Family Planning drive was launched it was first the Muslims who were forcibly made to undergo vasectomy operations, rendering them incapable of bearing children anytime in the future. When the party members of the non-Muslim extremist were imprisoned, the Jamat-e-Islami members, exemplary peaceful citizens, were also put into jails. When the situation prolonged, then, encouraged by others, and following his own instincts, Ali Miyan wrote a memorandum to Indira Gandhi and then personally went and met her. In his memorandum he reminded her of the constructive role that her father and grandfather had played in the past. He said that he was pretty sure that the imposition of the Emergency on the country was something she too didn't approve of in her heart, rather, she had been forced to take that extreme step.

He pointed out that perhaps it was without her knowledge that excesses were being committed against the people. He reminded her that the Indians looked at her not simply as a political figure, but rather as a mother of the nation. He was sure she didn't know what beastly methods were being adopted to force vasectomy on the citizens. They were being caught like ducks and operated on like chickens. He warned her that the goodwill that her family had built and gained over several generations could be lost in as many years and they might not be regained. During the conversation that followed, he also informed her that many people were remembering the good old British days when they felt less oppressed.

We do not know how Indira reacted to being referred as a mother, but, she was in power again a decade later, when the Muradabad attack on Muslims took place in which thousands lost their lives in the Prayer-Field. In fact, during her reign, Muslim lives were attacked no less in riots than at any other time. In 1977 however, when she had lost the election, she came down all the way to Nadwah to meet him. He tried to avoid seeing her, but she almost forced her entry in. He told her that he sympathized with her as a person wronged, since, he was sure she had been kept in dark over the gross injustices that were committed under the cover of Emergency imposed by her. A Muslim woman accompanying Indira broke into the conversation to chirp in that Ali Miyan should pray for Indira. He replied that he prayed for everyone who was truly devoted to the cause of the nation! One can imagine the face of a politician paid back in her own coins.

Interestingly, during the 19 months of the Emergency rule, it was Muslims alone who stood in protest and it was their voice alone that had reverberated in the halls and corridors of the government. The so-called patriots of the country who showed all signs of fanaticism in their display of patriotism in peace times, targeting and killing those who were truly patriotic towards the country, went into peaceful hybernation during the entire period, to come out of their slumber only after the Emergency was lifted. Once again they appeared in public as the true sons of India and ready to jump at the throats of the peaceful citizens! And, if they once again received a massive hearing, then one question - about the I.Q. of their followers - stood answered.

Notwithstanding their role during the Emergency, hatred against the Muslims was being spread by the tons in India, in consequence of which riots against them became the order of the day, not to speak of threats of new legislations every other day, with the view to forcibly incorporate the Muslims into Hinduism in the name of cultural assimilation, patriotism, national integration and so on. The situation forced Ali Miyan to taking greater and greater interests in socio-political affairs at home. The whirlwind let loose by the fanatics was too powerful to allow anyone escape its hold. Ali Miyan was so strongly drawn into it that - although brought up on a style of life more belonging to the world of the pen, books and the *khanqah* than of the tongue and the public platforms, he never thought of returning to the role his Sufi fore-fathers had played. Except that he did not participate in active politics, Ali Miyan went almost entirely public. Also, the field was empty. Important political and social figures who could give a lead in attempting to solve the problems of the *Ummah* had almost entirely disappeared. When the second-line leaders looked for someone who could chair their meetings, be it of literary, political, social, educational or of reformist nature, and scanned the length and breadth of India, the eyes rested on him. Not that he had emerged as the undisputed leader of the Indian Muslims, but that there were no contestants. Not that there were no scholars around.

 A few were still around. But they wouldn't play the role Ali Miyan was ready to play: what with traveling around the country and outside, spending the best part of the year in journeying from place to place. Others were either not interested, or did not have the energy, or were too busy with other pursuits to play this role. That was soon to be the situation to obtain in the Islamic world too. When the Arab ruling classes further tightened their iron grip on the Islamists, removing or imprisoning the first line leaders and the second line Arab leaders and field workers looked for someone to stand for Islamic causes, especially in the eighties and nineties and say something sensible from the podium, the choice fell on Ali Miyan.

Once again, not because he had outrun the rest. There were no rest: in the sense that a few left-overs were either not interested in the passive role or, were pretty sure what would happen to them if they spoke out point blank what should be spoken out. On his part Ali Miyan had perhaps realized - with special reference to India - that when the *Ummah*'s existence, and not simply identity, was being threatened, then articles and books were not the most urgent requirements. Accordingly, although he never gave up retreating to Takya Kalan for long or short spells, the demands of the community works brought him out and put him on the long road to seminars, travels, speeches during those years when his tired bones would have been calling for some relief.

Majlis-e-Mushawarat

His new role as one who called people to unite over social and moral issues, against the dangerous trends in life and society in a country under massive transmission, took him across the land addressing huge crowds (composed both of Muslims as well as non-Muslims). Wherever he and the delegates of the newly found "*Majlis-e-Mushawarat*" (Consultative Council) appeared, they touched on the hearts and sentiments of the people more than their minds and faculties of reason and logic. One such campaign alone took him across 4500 miles in the South of India. Things, however, didn't work well with the *Majlis-e-Mushawarat*.

It experienced a revival and cold storage effects, off and on, at short intervals. In the meanwhile, Ali Miyan felt that the Indian nation at large, composed of millions of Hindus, Sikhs, Christians, was also in need of people who could work against the slow but sure decline the country was facing in every field of activity and expression. The country's sure slide towards political, social and moral anarchy needed that all those who stood for sanity, moral integrity and reasonableness should join hands and try to rescue the nation. Following this urge Ali Miyan began giving fresh attention to the revival of his own movement "*Payam-e-Insaniyat*" (Message of Humanism) that he and Mawlana Manzoor No`mani had given birth to in 1954. It had been put into cold storage soon after. He revived it in 1974, although he was at that point without many able men that were available in 1954 and, moreover, the atmosphere was so poisoned with hatred of the Muslims, that many were very skeptic of its results. Some people even questioned the participation of Muslims in the movement, when the problem lay entirely with the majority community, and no Muslim gain seemed to be possible in the volatile and violent atmosphere that the extremists organizations had succeeded in creating.

Ali Miyan's point was that the Muslims being the torch-bearers of justice, human rights, moral integrity, equality, and service to the downtrodden, held the moral responsibility to work on these programs even if the dividends were poor. To the questions such as, when the situation in India was so horribly disheartening that students fell on class-mates with daggers, teachers attacked and killed colleagues of the same college - as in Jamshedpur - what could the victims, the Muslims, do in response? Ali Miyan replied that when there is fire, even the lame and the physically handicapped run to combat it. When a boat sinks then just about everyone sinks. If the majority community had lost its sense of balance, the common people were defying all moral restraints, and when the leaders of the country cared for nothing but power, wealth and influence, then, as a result, just about everyone was going to pay the price: the Muslims as well as the non-Muslims. It was a duty of the Muslims then, as bearers of a Message, to be the first to rise up in protest and make efforts at correction. Did they not have the Prophetic example before them who - before he was appointed a Messenger - had participated in the famous "*Hilf al-Fudul*" pact at Makkah that promised to help the helpless and obtained for the oppressed his right? If that was the Prophetic role in Makkan anarchy, that should be the Muslim role in Indian anarchy.

Payam-e-Insaniyyat

The mass meetings that were organized by the *Payam-e-Insaniyyat* movement to spread the message of tolerance, moral rectitude, patriotism, respect for human beings, honesty, integrity and sacrifice were well attended by the people. Surprisingly, a large number of non-Muslims attended the meetings. He reminded the non-Muslims that the best way of changing a man's attitudes and behavior was to make him God-conscious. That was sure to instill in him the fear of being held responsible one day by the Divinity. It was this power that transformed thieves into guardians. But, if that couldn't be attempted, and a movement of the kind he had launched, couldn't attempt to create God-consciousness, then the next best thing was to evoke feelings of patriotism. Social, economic, moral and political corruption had reached such levels as to threaten the very survival of India as one entity. The threads that were being pulled off then, would one day tear the cloth into shreds. The Muslims were also reminded that the sinking boat required everyone to plug every possible hole to save everyone, including those who made those holes, from sinking. Their responsibility in fact was two-fold. They were responsible to man, and, as Muslims, to Allah. Along with that both the communities were given a dose of hope by assuring that humanism was not dead. It was sleeping. It needed to be merely woken up. Presently, in the charged atmosphere, the situation was not normal. And, in that abnormal situation, nothing would work.

No number of universities – he said in a speech delivered in a University - would be any effective, if under the volatile and hostile situation, students were ready to jump on the throats of their benchmates. With this message he traveled through the whole of north India covering thousands of miles. In Chandigarh, (as in many other places) the meeting was presided by a non-Muslim. When he spoke at length, repeating what he had been saying all along, the huge mass of men present, mostly Sikhs and Hindus, sat in complete silence. When some Muslims (who were but a few there) wanted to leave the gathering, the non-Muslims pulled them down saying they wouldn't hear those beautiful words too often.

Between 1974 and 1980, Ali Miyan gave the movement whole six years. But, as he admitted, the movement could not create a second line leadership. Although non-Muslims participated in mass meetings, none ever came forward to move the movement. If any non-Muslim spoke, after Ali Miyan had spoken to soften the hearts, he only advised the Muslims to reform themselves, and join the mainstream, meaning, Hindu stream, meaning, turn Hindus. Ali Miyan thought the situation with them was pathetic. While hundreds of newly-wed Hindu girls were being burned to death every month for not having brought enough dowry, and the society suffered from some very serious ailments and moral failures that threatened the balanced life of the country-men, Hindus and Muslims alike, the Hindus only perceived Muslims as the main threat to the country.

Whatever the other effects of his movement, especially aimed at the non-Muslims, it is curious to note that at the end of six years of hard work in 1980, a huge attack on the Muslim lives took place in Muradabad. Ali Miyan's "mother of the nation" was then the Prime Minister. The day chosen was that of 'Eid, and the place the open Prayer ground ('*Eid-gah* where Muslims offer yearly Prayers).

Another specialty of this attack on Muslims was the murder of small children who had come in their best attires closed to attend the Prayers. On a small pretext the police opened fire killing some 2000 Muslims on the spot, in the Prayer ground. The number of children killed was 700. Next day onwards for a few days, it was a free killing of Muslims, burning, looting and destruction of their property and industries. A city where Muslims dominated in the handicraft business, Muradabad was reduced to ashes in a few days. The whole thing, so well-planned and so well-executed, appeared as an answer to Ali Miyan's "Message of Humanism" movement. Aligarh, Banaras, Meerut, Alahabad and Bhiwandi were other cities where the Muslims controlled some business or industry, and where later similar messages of "acceptance" were delivered to the "Message of Humanism" movement. As usual, another convention of the Muslims was held, a few speeches made, a few suggestions offered, some resolutions passed, the government reminded of its responsibilities, and some encouraging remarks of a few Hindus obtained, and – as Ali Miyan wrote - what more could be done?!

Vande Mataram

The "acceptance" of his "Message of Humanism" was once again demonstrated when in 1993 the police entered the Nadwahtul Ulama, of which Ali Miyan was the honory rector, at night, broke furniture and beat up the students. They were looking for supposed Kashmiri Mujahideen. As a final honor, extremist hooligans went one step further and entered Takya Kalan in 1996, in particular looking for the 80 year old Ali Miyan, for the reasons that he had made a statement that the Muslims will never sing "Vande Mataram," a poem steeped in polytheistic concepts. Luckily Ali Miyan wasn't at home. The majority community, especially those who came to power walking over pools of blood, seemed to have well understood his message and were responding in ways their own light of guidance showed them as the path to Heaven.

Late Years

The Faisal Award

In 1980 Ali Miyan received the prestigious Islamic Faisal Award, which he hadn't expected since he had recently written a memorandum to the rulers of Saudi Arabia, expressing his fears that the country would be seriously affected by its drive to modernism, losing its Islamic character in its development efforts, especially in view of the purposeless life of its citizens fed on film and football. *Sheikh al-Hadith*, Mawlana Zakariyyah was alive and residing in Madinah. Aware of Ali Miyan's nature of rejecting honors and awards, he sent him the message that the award could be accepted. Ali Miyan nominated Dr. Abdullah Abbas Nadwi to receive the award at Makkah and give away half the amount (about 200,000 Saudi Riyals) to the Afghan Jihad, and twenty-five percent each to two Qur'anic and religious *Madrasas* in Saudi Arabia itself.

In 1981 he was awarded a doctorate degree by the Kashmir University, where the chairman of the convocation, B.K. Nehru was so moved by his speech that he stood up to say that he had never heard any such talk in any of the several convocations that he had attended. The content of the speech was that humanizing an individual should be the aim, and character-building the objective of any educational system. He pointed out that the principles of a civilized life were respect for the human being, self-control, preference of collective interests over personal interests, protection of human life, property and honor, protection of the poor and the oppressed, the will to face the usurpers of human rights, fearlessness before those who cared for nothing but power and wealth, the courage to speak out the truth even if against one's kin, race and nation, justice for all, and the fear of being watched and reckoned by a Supreme Power. These are the qualities that allowed a person to be considered called as civilized. The educational system should be designed to inculcate such qualities. Obviously, a call of this nature had not been heard in a University Hall since the universities had come to exist.

The year 1981 also saw him participating in an Algerian yearly religious Seminar. That the authorities did not wish him get too close to the youth was quite clear. Early in February the next year he was in Sri Lanka, to preside over the convocation of the first graduates of the Nazimia College at Colombo. It was set up by a diamond merchant Nazimi who had taken the step eight years ago after being influenced by Ali Miyan's "*An Apostasy that has no Abu Bakr to Combat.*" Built entirely at his cost, the University was awarding degrees to its first batch of graduates. In 1982 when Beirut was under siege, and such crimes were committed by the Israelites, the Phalangists and Maronite Christians as which put the humanity to shame - Palestinians were tied to two jeeps by their legs and the vehicles driven apart to split them into two - he wrote a strong article that someone in Chicago translated and sent a copy to Ronald Reagan, the then President of the United States on whose backing the crimes against the Palestinians were committed. Otherwise too the article received a wide circulation.

At home, and despite his chronic gout problem, Ali Miyan remained busy attending seminars, conventions and mass meetings. He participated in an All-India Seminar on "Arabic Language: its teaching and problems" held at Hyderabad in 1982. Once in the city, he delivered lectures in various places. In one of his lectures he pointed out that the decline of a nation begins with its moral decline. Greek, Roman, Sassanid, were some of those civilizations of the past that gradually slid into oblivion when they paid no attention to their moral decline. The situation in India was the same now. It was obvious that the only thing that mattered in the country was money, caste, lucrative jobs, high-posts and political power.

Nothing else mattered. From one end of the country to another end, there was not a single protest over what was happening, not a single voice raising a moral issue. Nobody ever gave a call to save humanism, morals, and the country. All that one could hear was, "Join our ranks and take up our issue, right or wrong. Accept our hegemony." The country was fast heading towards self-destruction.

In another session, he reminded the religiously committed that no amount of personal piety would be enough to save the Muslims from destruction unless they took interest in their surroundings. If political, social, economic and moral problems were not addressed, soon the Muslims would face problems - not of leadership role - but in offering their Prayers. If they remained oblivious of the rights of the country on them, they'd soon discover that their mosques were under threat.

Oxford University

In 1983 he was invited by the Oxford University to attend the founding of the Islamic Center there. He was made the chairman of the institution. In his address he complained that although the West had created great minds in the past, such as those who changed the ways of the world, especially in the fields of science and technology, it was now passing through a static stage unable to produce men who could exercise good influence on the society. The West also failed to give a constructive turn to the scientific and technological developments. Before starting to travel to Oxford, he had wished to be able to address a good assembly of non-Muslim Western intellectuals, specialists and experts and press a message on them, which either it was never delivered to them in the past, or, if delivered, superiority complex and a sense of achievement, had come in the way of serious consideration. That was his main objective in his travel to Britain. But, as things should happen, neither was the targeted audience there in numbers he had wished, nor, one would say, the message was powerful enough - being clothed in easternism - to influence those it reached. Translation reduced the power of speech to invisible levels.

The same year he also traveled on invitation to Sharjah, Dubai and Kuwait, as usual addressing huge gatherings and reminding various classes of people of their duties towards Islam, the society they lived in and the humanity at large. In one speech he stressed on the need to construct a fully committed Muslim society on a wholly Islamic pattern, as a model for the rest of the world.

While in the seventieth year of his life in 1984, Ali Main received a pressing invitation from the Royal family of Jordan to attend a conference to be held in Amman (Jordan) by the "Islamic Civilization Research Academy." Well attended by delegates from 32 Islamic countries, including some from Moscow (headed by Baba Khanov), the conference was dominated by Prince Hasan's speech in which he highlighted the gravity of the problems Jordan was facing in its confrontation with Israel. With the help of maps and charts, and a large amount of data, he put the audience into an uncomfortable spell by demonstrating the realities of the Israeli occupation and its future plans.

In his turn Ali Miyan pointed out that history tells us that when facing difficult situations, it is the will and determination of a people which finally counts. The enemy might create an impossible situation, realities that strongly reflect on maps and charts, but once the challenge is answered with a challenge, and a determined people stand up, ready to sacrifice all that they posses, face up to any difficulty that they are confronted with, then the facts and figures, data on maps and charts, and the huge numbers, along with their equipments, melt away like wax under the heat of the people's determination. The impossible then becomes possible. The night is pierced by the light of the unstoppable day. This is what history teaches us, especially from the example of Sultan Salahuddin Ayyubi. Dr. Iqbal had well illustrated this fact in a couplet:

If there is a Kaleem (Musa) in confrontation
Then, even now you can hear from Mount Tur, `fear not.'
Master Rumi's companionship has revealed to me that
A hundred thousand heads in prostration are unequal to a Kaleem in combat.

The speech seemed to have restored warmth to the hearts and moistened a few eyes among the audience.

In another speech at the College of Arabic, he emphasized the need for the Muslims to retain their identity as Muslims, which was only possible if they drew inspiration from Islam. That would give them the power that had overcome the highly developed Roman and Persian civilizations, despite their material powers.

He also visited the caves of the Seven Sleepers (*As-hab al Kahaf*). Rafeeq Wafa Dijjani's research work, which was done for his doctorate degree, had strongly demonstrated that the caves located eight km. down south of Amman, are those very caves wherein a few young men took refuge and were put to sleep by Allah for three centuries. Excavations had led to findings of several tablets bearing the names "*Al-Raqeem* Cave." The cave has eight graves and agrees with several Qur'anic details. Of the historians of old, Maqdisi, Al-Bayruni and Yaqut also indicated that these were the caves spoken of in the Qur'an. From among the Orientalists, one or two have also agreed with the findings and the identity of the caves. Until Rafiq Wafa Dijjani's findings, it was widely believed that the caves were in present day Turkey, sixty km. from Azmir (Anatolia).

In the Tablighee center of Amman he expressed the need for the Da`wa workers, to maintain high moral and spiritual standards with the help of supererogatory acts. But they ought not to forget to study and understand in greater detail the religion of Islam. They must also keep an eye on the events of the world and the developing situations, with special reference to currents that affect the Islamic boat. He quoted Iqbal again:

If you do not know the realities of this life
Your glass will not be able to face the stones.

In one of the private sessions, the question of how to deal with the Muslim rulers came up and the prevalent opinion was that there was no wisdom in confrontation.

His journey was planned via Makkah and Madinah. A delegation of leading writers and intellectuals came to him seeking his approval to set up a "Literary Forum" which was to have its headquarters in Nadwah, Lucknow, with Rabi` Nadwi as its first general secretary. Headed by Ali Miyan, it was to invite writers from all over the world to register in and then organize meetings at regular intervals.

In Yemen

From Hejaz he traveled to Yemen. From the airport (then North Yemen), he was first taken, following Yemeni wisdom, to a scholar's house in the countryside. What with the old hut-like house, with goats in the yard, it was to impress on `Ali Miyan how the Yemeni scholars lived: untouched by modern material comforts in contrast to the royal life enjoyed by a few scholars in other parts of the world. The scholar at the moment was Sheikh Yasin `Abd al-`Aziz. He expressed his opinion that there were two methods of bringing meaningful and lasting changes in an Islamic polity. First, believers "should occupy the seats of power," and second, "take faith to those who occupy the seats of power." The Sheikh himself believed in the second method. Ali Miyan agreed with him and mentioned the example of Mujaddid Alf-Thani, who brought revolutionary changes by "taking the message" to those in the seats of power, rather than try to occupy those seats. It was possible that Ali Miyan was being told how to deal with this issue when he met with the Yemeni rulers. On various other occasions during his stay, he found the Yemeni wisdom at work.

He found that three writers were popularly read in Yemen: himself, Mawlana Mawdudi and Sayyid Qutb, and to good effect. For example, when the communist South Yemeni forces launched an attack on the North Yemen, penetrating deep and occupying some strategic areas, and it was being believed that if they kept pressing on, the whole of the North would be lost to communist forces and communism, it was a few young men who requested that they be armed and allowed to fight on a voluntary basis. Equipped with a few tanks and other lighter equipment, they launched a counteroffensive from the mountains and ultimately pushed back the communist forces. In fact, the Islamists played the central role in the unification of the two Yemens.

Shah Waliyullah

In 1984 he brought out the fifth volume of "*Saviors of Islamic Spirit*" consisting of the life of Shah Waliyullah. Whether or not the most important figure in Islam after Ibn Taymiyyah - as considered by some - or even more important than him from certain angles, as Ali Miyan said, Shah Waliyullah certainly played a very important role in the reconstruction of Islamic thought in the Indian sub-continent. He and his four sons, Shah `Abdul Qadir, Shah `Abdul Aziz, Shah Rafiuddin and Shah `Abdul Ghani revived interest in religion and gave it a new impetus.

Most subsequent religious activities after them are attributed to their influences that are said to last to this day. Their efforts at popularizing the study of the Qur'an and Sunnah, seek for the true meaning beyond the surface of the words, seek food both for thought as well as for practical actions, in addition to their interests in Jihad activities revived not only the religious sciences but also inspired men of conviction to, on the one hand, set up religious institutions, wage a struggle against the *Ahl al-bid`ah*, establish the *Sunnah*, and, on the other, fight the enemy out in the battle-field and lay lives for moral causes - if it came to that.

Also in 1984 when Indira Gandhi was murdered and a massive killing operation was launched against the Sikhs, especially in New Delhi, where some 500 Sikhs were killed overnight, many burned to death, their business looted, and some of the looted material reached Takya Kalan and its surrounding villages, presumably through Muslim hands, then Ali Miyan issued a simple statement: "diseases will visit those homes where the looted materials have arrived." Very soon the sentence spread around and Muslims began to restore the goods to the Sikh owners. In response, Sikhs came to him and with tears in their eyes, some of them touching his feet, thanked him for the stand he had taken.

(However, it might not be missed to note that if, inspired by the Hindu initiative, some Muslims indulged in looting Sikh shops, there were many more who actually sheltered the Sikhs and their families in their homes and saved them from being murdered. This, despite the fact that the Sikhs had never in the past let an opportunity go by without harming the Muslim. The Sikhs are yet to say sorry for their historic role, and yet to say thanks in practical terms for the Muslim role during the Delhi riots.

Shah Banu Case

The year 1985 proved to be another eventful year for the Muslims of India. That was the year when the Supreme Court passed a judgement over the famous Shah Banu case, ordering Muslim men to bear the maintenance cost of their divorced wives, though of course a clause made it conditional to the husband's affordability. The court also recommended the formation and implementation of a common civil code for all Indian citizens, regardless of their faith.

This was of course entirely against the Islamic principles and, moreover, a measure of oppression against Muslim women. Islamic law says that after divorce the father, or, in his absence, his brother(s) and others of the family-members of the father's side on the male line, are responsible for the maintenance of a husband-less woman. And, they are bound to provide her food, shelter, clothing and medicine, whether the father, brother(s) and others happen to be rich or poor. Further, they are bound to provide for her, in all cases, whether the husband divorced her, or died.

Finally, the father, brother(s) are bound to provide for her, whether the woman herself happens to be rich or poor, employed or not. But the court ruling, speciously kind on her, actually did Muslim women great wrong by asking the former husband pay for her maintenance, on condition of affordability. If he was poor, he was not bound. That meant in fact that a Muslim woman got nothing in actual fact since, according to Indian governmental statistics, 80% of Indians and among them greater number of Muslims live below the poverty line. Further, if the court ruling was accepted, while it would have been a harrowing job for 10% of Muslim women to get maintenance from their former husbands, the rest of the 90% would be deprived of their right of maintenance from their parents, not to speak of the deprivation in case of the husband's death, or the wife seeking separation.

Muslims of the whole country stood up against the ruling as one man. It was obvious that it was a testing case. If the Muslims didn't rise on that occasion in protest, in the next steps the whole of the *Shari`ah* would be declared null and void. The Shi`a, Bohris, Barelawis, Mehdawis, everyone rose up in protest.

Protest gatherings were organized all over India, in every city and town, that were so well attended in hundreds of thousands as to leave even the speakers spell-bound. (The honest Indian press reported the gatherings, if it ever reported, as of a few thousand). And, what was notable is that although hundreds of such protests gatherings were organized by the All India Muslim Personal Law Board, of which Ali Miyan was the chairman, not a single one went violent. Muslims proved that at the national level they were an exemplary community, from whom the non-Muslims had plenty to learn. Despite having entered into his seventies, Ali Miyan, along with Mawlana Mujahid al-Islam Qasmi, organized protest mass meetings all over the South of India. When the delegates passed by smaller towns during the course of their train journeys, they discovered that huge crowds were waiting for them at the railway platforms at midnight, eager to register the message that just about every single Indian Muslim was behind them in their fight against the attack on their religious laws.

Muslim Women

Most surprisingly, the Muslim-haters did not seem to have played their card well. Although seemingly they had tried to evoke Muslim women against Islam by their show of sympathy for them, it was Muslim women who stood up in massive protest all over India. Amazingly, as if in proof that Indian Muslims could not be written off as those who did not care for their religion, it was the educated Muslim women who rose up in protest against the oppressive court ruling. Led by Begum Abida Ahmed, Najma Heptullah, Begum Ziar-Rahman Ansari, Begum Khurshid Alam Khan, Begum Sagher Nizami, and many others, Muslim women came out in surprising numbers and spoke with amazing conviction against the court ruling and the intended common civil code bill. That must have been very disappointing for those who had thought they would divide the Muslims over the issue.

The Press and other media felt hurt as if they had been stabbed in their guts. They came out as one unit, one body and one soul, in opposition to the Muslims' opposition. Newspapers were full of vindictive articles against Islam and Muslims, and so much attention was paid to the affair as if it was the question of India's survival as a nation, or maybe there had been an earthquake accompanied by lava eruptions all over India. By over-reacting to the issue, the Press, inadvertently removed the veil of secularism from its face. That was a good lesson for those modern educated but simple Muslims who believed that they lived in a secular India, where the Press was entirely neutral. The over-reaction was a good thing to happen to many

Muslims to realize who their true friends were. They were not outside of the boundaries of the community.

Sati

Interestingly, those very days when 700 Hindu women were being burned to death every year by their in-laws in Delhi alone, for not bringing enough cash or property from their parents at marriage, a Hindu woman Rup Kanwar committed self-immolation (Sati) in front of 600,000 wild men and women, dancing in praise of the revival of the age-old Hindu custom. The Press however, seemed to have forgotten the cause of the "down-trodden women – especially Muslim women" and hardly bothered to devote an editorial to it. In a country where, according to Time of India of 6th April 1986, 6.6 million illegal abortions take place yearly. Most are those that involve female fetuses. In this background, the attention the media gave to the Shah Banu case was surely as courageous an act, as curious.

In any case, when the Bill was presented to the Government, Muslim leaders stood up as one body, played their cards well and sought to nullify it with the help of a few clauses, so that, even if passed by the parliament, the effectiveness would be removed. Fully convinced that the entire Muslim population was opposed to any move towards tampering with their *Shari`ah*, Rajiv Gandhi, the then Prime Minister, played the whole thing out very cleverly to get the Bill passed with the proposed amendments although the opposition made a big noise in the parliament until the late hours of the night when the voting was conducted.

Having experienced the poison in the press, radio and TV against the Muslims, Ali Miyan felt that it was extremely important to exchange opinions with important members of the majority community. Accordingly, dialogue-sessions were organized in several towns and cities of Central India, notably Nagpur, where RSS has its headquarters, Poona, which is considered a seat of Hindu revival as well as in Delhi. Attended and appreciated by many leading Hindu intellectuals and renowned figures such as Inder Kumar Gujral (former ambassador to Russia), Kuldip Nayar (the well-known journalist), Malik Ram, Chand Sarkar (Vice-Chancellor Nagpur University), Agwal Tawde, S.D. Wagh (Editor, *Maharashtra Herald*), and several others demonstrated through their participation and speeches that the powerful hooliganism had not reached the intellectual class yet. While in one meeting a Hindu speaker said - in explanation of the Islamo-phobia that the Hindus suffered - that the Hindus felt threatened in this country both from without, being surrounded by Muslim states, as well as from within, faced up with the growing Muslim population, Ali Miyan on the other hand pointed out that anarchy could not meet anarchy without the two destroying each other. Nor could united fronts meet head on with united fronts without the two getting injured. It wasn't also possible for those not directly involved to look in another direction while someone was poking a dagger into another innocent being. He informed the mixed Hindu-Muslim audience that if the upper class (read upper-caste), travelers in a boat denied water to the lower deck travelers and did not object to their drilling a hole in the bottom of the boat, both would sink.

The Gulf War

Saddam Hussain's adventure into Kuwait in 1990 created a situation of emergency and took Ali Miyan to Saudi Arabia to participate in a meeting organized to seek the consensus of the world scholars over the American forces that had already arrived into the country. There, and at various other forums in India, `Ali Miyan openly condemned the Iraqi regime and, considering Arab nationalism as the root cause of religious decline, social imbalances, material backwardness and political turmoil. He wrote several articles for an Urdu magazine "*Ta`mir-e-Hayat,*" criticizing the Arabs in no concealed words. The events also prompted him to write a letter to King Fahd of Saudi Arabia in which he pointed out that two primary constituents were missing from the Islamic world: i) a living model of an Islamic society, and ii) a powerful Islamic leadership that could face up the challenges of the time. It was lack of the former that had prevented the spread of Islamic call, and that of the latter that had led the youth to respond with enthusiasm to any call that challenged the West, however hollow the challenge happened to be. Therefore, it was the crying need of the time to respond to these two pressing needs. He thought the king was in a position both to take steps that would create the model Islamic community as well as personally assume the role of leadership of the Islamic world in the footsteps of `Umar b. `Abdul `Aziz! The king wrote him back that he was fully aware of the need and the challenge, as well as of the fact that it was only return to the Qur'an and Sunnah and the good example set by the renowned men of Islam that guaranteed salvation to the Islamic world!

Another Letter

When Narasimha Rao became the Prime Minister of India, Ali Miyan wrote to him his customary letter warning him of the depravity to which the country had fallen, the corruption that had boomeranged in the administration, and the moral degradation to which the masses had sunk. Another contemporary evil deserved special attention. It was the wide recourse to violence which was fueled by hatred being freely distributed by the tons. Stories that were several centuries old, and which had probably no historical basis, were being dug up from the archives, or cooked up anew, to spread hatred against a section of the people and incite violence against them.

Whatever else Rao did, (many people were convinced that he had a role in the demolition of the Babari Mosque), in response to Ali Miyan's letter, but at least he spoke to him over the telephone to offer him the Padma Bhushan award. But, following his principle, 'Ali Miyan declined to accept the honor. In 1992 Rao also wrote to him (by his own hand in eloquent Urdu) to come and meet him at Delhi and work out a formula acceptable both to the Muslims as well as the Hindu fundamentalists who had vowed the destruction of the Mosque. But, Ali Miyan realized the danger involved in meeting politicians on their grounds, and preferred to see him in the company of the "Babari Masjid Action Committee" in order not to be led into a situation where he would have to bear the responsibility for the unpredictable events.

The Babari Masjid

Finally, on the 6th of December 1992, preceded by open rehearsals of the demolition, the Babari mosque was demolished, in front of the TV cameras, and with full co-operation of the government security forces. (Respectable historians like Dr. R.L.Shukla and Chanandas Gupta have shown that there never was a temple in place of the Babari Masjid). The demolition led to protests by the Muslims which largely remained peaceful. But the security forces retaliated in the most brutal manner. As a result, tens of thousands of Muslims were martyred and millions of dollars of their property destroyed in a couple of days. Not only the police and the security forces, but also the para-military organizations seemed to be acting on a plan. They were sure of the demolition, confident of the protests, and sure of what they would do and when. With the security forces attending to their honorable task, and with the cover provided by them, those that had been trained over half a century how to attack, loot and plunder on short notice, took charge. In the days of complete chaos that followed, all limits of humanity were crossed, in the open, without any majority community organization raising a single voice of protest. In some places, Muslim women were raped in the streets while cameras made films.

Subsequently, they were shot dead.

Ali Miyan was unable to account for the violence against those who were only protesting - peacefully - over an illegal act. Unable to explain, and, perhaps finding the truth too bitter for verbal expression, all that he could think was that the Indians were probably passing through a phase of madness. Otherwise, he did not know how to explain the massive all-India killing, burning, loot, plunder, throwing of children on the tracks of running trains, cutting humans into pieces and various other more horrendous acts of violence. In a speech, perhaps the longest of his life, he betrayed his confusion. Was all that he had been saying, for fifty years, a pleasant but deluding philosophy? Merely fashionable words? Was his faith in the ultimate goodness of the humans wrongly placed?

Was humanity, as he so often said, merely sleeping, or wolves lived side by side, deep in the souls of those who outwardly and incessantly expressed their faith in peaceful living, and swore by non-violence, but that only when they were not busy organizing riots? These were perhaps difficult questions for him to answer. And his speech, which was closer to being a long harangue, betrayed the disquiet of his mind. Although he still found, perhaps, grounds to hold on to his philosophy of hope, he could not, at the same time, be as forceful in his call to reason, logic and goodness. For the first time his mind seemed to be thinking whether retaliation was truly so silly as to be ruled out? But, in keeping with the softness of his character, he only ended by reminding the government that if the Muslim holy places were taken away from them forcibly, then, hadn't the Jains and Buddhists the right to demand back thousands of their places of worship that had been forcibly taken away from them in the southern Indian regions, by the Shankaracharya in the eighth century? He also reminded his audience that India could survive as one nation only if it remained democratic, secular, and non-violent.

It was a disorganized speech, betraying the depth to which Ali Miyan was disturbed by the country-wide, well directed violence and the cruelty with which it was executed. He just couldn't believe that his countrymen - in whom he had great faith - could on short notice become wolves and sink their teeth on Muslim necks at no provocation, and later, appear completely normal, as if their teeth weren't red with blood. He didn't know which was a greater tragedy: the demolition of the Babari Mosque which had degraded Indians over the globe, or, the unprovoked violence against Muslims, which had led peoples of many nations to a reassessment of the Indian majority community's true character, and the nature of the religion they professed to follow.

An inquiry commission set up by the government said in its report of the December 13th that the demolition of the Babari Mosque was carried out by the Sangh Parivar and the responsibility lay with the provincial and the central government which were fully aware of their intentions and preparations. The security forces at the time of demonstration stood motionless as mute witnesses to the event. Although we do not know the legal worth, or in fact, whether it has been proven in a court of law or not, but it was reported that Justice Achniya Reddy, Justice D.S. Tiwatia and others named Lal Krishnan Advani, Murali Manohar Joshi, Ashok Singhal, Vijay Rajay Scindhia, Vinay Katyar, Uma Bharati and various others as those who were involved in various operations at various stages. These were the very ones who were to form the government later, riding high on popularity gained through these achievements. They would hold ministerial positions related to law and order in the country. When that happened, then all that Ali Miyan could say was that these people had demonstrated that when a people make up their minds to do something, and work on it consistently, they finally achieve their goals! (He had meant political gains). He said nothing about those Indians who had placed their trust in this class of people, and had voted them into power for the sole reason that they hated the Muslims. Did their trust in known lawbreakers say something about the need for a redefinition of their own personality, culture and ethos?

Although little did the majority community realize, and actually distributed sweets in the Gulf countries in celebration of the demolition, they paid a huge price in dignity for the barbarian act. In the Middle-East, where they were respected for their hard-work and professionalism, they suddenly became a lowly assessed people. What respect and honor the nation had achieved in fifty years, especially in the non-aligned circles, it lost in a day. But the most ironic aspect was that there were little signs that the lesson was learned. The efforts to deface Hinduism, continued under the impression that covert actions will never be brought to light and so, do not promise the same consequences.

Payam-e-Insaniyyat Again

All said, felt, questioned and answered, Ali Miyan was not to give up. He stuck to his moral guns. In 1993 he organized another convention of the "Message of Humanity." This time it was in Patna (Bihar). Chief Minister Laloo Prasad Yadav presided. Others present were Dr. Jagan Nath Misra, Micoram (IGP), S.K.Sinha (Retd. Army General), Father Paul Jackson (a leading Church representative), Major Balbir Singh, Chief Secretary of the Bihar government, and other dignitaries. In his talk Ali Miyan repeated what he had been saying about the importance of democracy, secularism and non-violence, and expressed his concern over the prevalent excessive love of wealth that led the Indians to many ignoble acts.

He informed his audience that he was personally so ashamed of the ruthless and massive attack on Muslim lives and property that he had decided against attending the "World Muslim League" conference at Makkah in fear that if asked, he would have to speak out the truth which would only earn the Indians shame and humiliation. So, Ali Miyan's mind was after all working in the direction of redefinition and reassessment. However, there was now a fundamental change. His Muslim audience were ahead of him in his reassessments. But they had reached conclusions that did not seem to be his conclusions. Many wondered if there was any point in talking on those lines. Some of his linesmen were quite ready to quit all such efforts, and millions of the laity were with them.

A few other Responses

Whatever the effects of his talk on the so-called responsible section of the Hindus, a few things did happen that couldn't be counted out as mere coincidences. The first was the storm in Rae-Bareli, a Congress citadel. Huge preparations were made to conduct a meeting in which top class Congress workers were to meet. Taking place immediately after the demolition of the Babari Mosque, with the feverishness and joy demonstrated in the preparations, it appeared as a meeting in celebration of the destruction. But, one day before the jubilant Congress Party members could climb the stage behind the Prime Minister Narasimha Rao, the town experienced a massive tornado. It was something very rare for the geographical area. The preparations of months were destroyed in minutes. Everything was blown away - *Ghazwah Khandaq* like. The losses were estimated at 500 million.

A second event was the earthquake that struck in south of India, centering in at a place called Lathur. Few people outside the region knew where Lathur was. But Muslims knew it pretty well. It was the hot-bed of BJP and Shiv Sena. It was from here that seven truck loads of volunteers (Kar Sewaks) were sent to participate in the demolition of the Babri Mosque. Send-off parties were arranged by maddening crowds that displayed uncontrolled frenzy while dispatching Kar Sevaks to the holy task. It was from this place that a gold brick was sent for the construction of the proposed Ram Temple in place of the Babari Mosque. And it was here that on 11th of November of the year 1993 a massive earthquake struck two hours before dawn. What happened was an eye opener for Hindus and Muslims alike. While the whole area was reduced to rubble, including a Temple built out of concrete, and so too a Bank building, a loner stood its ground proud among the rubble. It was a mosque. Even Qur'an copies in the open racks and niches had not toppled down, while the buildings around the mosque lay flat on their roofs. Khilari, another anti-Muslim town nearby, was also completely flattened. But that was not all. Some 52 towns and villages had been flattened. In an area of mixed population, where the Muslims were massacred in great numbers at the time of (Hyderabad) Police Action in 1948, the earthquake took the life of some 77,000 people. Strangely however, Muslims suffered marginal losses. They lost a total of 1080 lives. After the earth-quake the first to reach the spot were Shiv Sena workers along with the police. The first thing they did - so alleged the locals - was to rob the dead of their gold and cash.

In keeping with his principles, Ali Miyan would not believe in the published stories until he traveled to nearby Bombay for a few days rest and as an escape maneuver from the elections in North India. There he received eye-witness accounts from extremely trustworthy sources. Interestingly, when some religious, political and community leaders went to inspect the area after the earthquake, those very people who had organized on their orders the seven truck-load of men for Babari Mosque destruction abused them and told them to stay away from the area altogether. The place being hundreds of miles away from the fault lines, no geologist could have predicted an earthquake of that magnitude. A university Hindu teacher traveling with his students told them that there was good grounds to connect the earthquake with the destruction of the mosque.

A third incident that could have acted as an eye-opener for the political leaders at the center, if they had any eyes, was that of plague that struck another famous anti-Muslim region: Gujarat. It centered on the town of Surat: the town where Muslim women were paraded naked in the streets during the riots that followed the destruction of the mosque. The townspeople had committed other atrocities during their attack on Muslim lives, honor and property. The plague, which struck in September 1994, divided the town into two sections: the Muslim and non-Muslim. The Muslim areas – ghettos - remained unaffected. The non-Muslim area was clearly the target of the rats. As a result, the posh area of the town was emptied of its inhabitants in a few days. Thousands died, and many more ran away. A few Hindus were quick at learning the lesson. Two of the mosques that had stopped functioning after the attack on Muslims in Dec. 1993, were re-opened on Hindu request. Hundreds of people were seen trekking to the Muslim grave-yard, going down on their knees at the graves and seeking their forgiveness for what was done to them in December 1993. Non-Muslim elitists were thronging the slums for amulets from the Muslim Charm workers.

(Strangely, in 2001 Gujarat was struck with a massive earthquake.

The richest state of the country, the largest exporter, was reduced to rubble. In terms of human and material losses, India hadn't recorded a calamity of this magnitude since its independence. But, greater than the losses due to an earthquake, little do the Gujaratis realize what it means now to be referred to as a Gujarati).

A Long Journey

Ali Miyan was about 80 years old in 1994 when he made the longest journey of his life, attending various conferences in Turkey, UK, USA, Switzerland, and, finally, Makkah and Madinah. He returned to India to carry on with his "Message of Humanism" through conventions and assemblies. Several large gatherings were held in different parts of the country with some non-Muslim cabinet ministers attending them. But, apparently, to some, a suitable reply was needed to counter his activities. It came in the form of a raid on Nadwah by the intelligence bureau in December 1994. They came at midnight, broke their own rule of not raiding any students' residential quarters without first contacting the Principle or Warden of the educational institution. The raiding party locked the rooms of several hostels from outside, and then forced open a room of one of the hostels, arresting several inmates. When a few others emerged from the unlocked rooms and protested the arrest, the security forces opened fire, injuring some. The interrogation of the arrested students, however, proved nothing: they were as innocent as butterflies and were later unconditionally released. When a protest was launched by the institution for not taking the head of the institution into confidence before the raid, Nadwah was awarded US$ 4500 as compensation, which it declined to accept. The message the totally unwarranted police raid was quite clear: "You are not safe anywhere in this country no matter how clear your record."

With age advancing on him, Ali Miyan was getting less active. But not so inactive as not to answer pressing invitations. Although in 1995 he avoided going to Sudan for a conference, twice he made to South India, in addition to journeys to central Indian towns: Aurangabad, Nagpur, Bombay and even to the Gulf. However, when invited by the "Muslim Universities' Federation" to attend its conference in Cairo in May 1995, he begged excuse on health grounds and sent one of his deputies. The report that the deputy later brought back from Egypt, detailed both religious oppression on a massive scale, as well as cause for hope. It said that in Egypt some 70-80,000 religious men were in prisons. Religiously inclined youth were being engaged in false encounters and shot dead. Mosque courtyards and open spaces in front of them where hundreds of thousands of Egyptians traditionally assembled for 'Eid Prayers were being inundated with water and roads leading to mosques lined up with tanks preventing entry. No religious assembly was possible. Ikhwan's social and economic activities too were being curtailed: some of their financial institutions had been sold to the Jews. Imams read out sermons prepared by governmental authorities. Most institutional course books had been emptied of any critical reference to the Jews and Christians. Early Islamic war stories had been replaced with the stories of the Pharoah dynasty, and all Qur'anic verses referring to the Jews removed from the school and college text books.

The hope contained in the fact that despite the oppressive measures, religiosity seemed to be on the rise. More and more women were donning modest dresses. Some fifteen percent of them were wearing the Indian type of Burqah complete with Niqab covering their faces and the outfit complete with socks and hand-gloves. Bookstores selling Islamic books had vastly increased in numbers and Islamic books were in great. Ali Miyan's book "*Ma Dha...*" had been reprinted by no less than five Egyptian publishers and was doing well on the stands. His recent "*Al-Murtada*" being the life of `Ali ibn Abi Talib had received praise from a person no less than Gaad al-Haq, the Rector of Azhar University and read out on the Egyptian radio. Several of his other works were being popularly read by Egyptians of all classes. His "*Stories of the Prophets*" was being increasingly adopted by Egyptian schools and nurseries. One of the Egyptian reformers, `Abd al-Karim Sulayman had in fact set up a *Da`wah* institute where quite a few of his works were prescribed as course books.

By 1996 Ali Miyan had not only acquired international fame, but within India too, where the majority community normally ignores Muslim leaders, he was receiving acknowledgment. Deve Gowda (the first and until now the only non-Brahmin Prime Minister of India), who had been freshly elected as a Prime Minister of a coalition government at the center, paid a short visit to him at Lucknow. Reacting to it, the BJP issued a statement that the visit only strengthened the anti-social and anti-national elements in the country! The party spokesman also said that the two great educational institutions, Deoband and Nadwah, were both centers of Pakistani intelligence operations. In his response to the unexpected visit, Ali Miyan later wrote his customary letter to the Prime Minister reminding him that ultimately what succeeded was sincerity, honesty and truthfulness. He also reminded him that the past great leaders of India had built this country on the principles of democracy, secularism and non-violence. Any action by those in power in neglect of these principles would only destroy what had already been built.

At the end of the year 1995 he attended the annual conference of the "World Muslim League" held in Makkah. He had decided to attend in the hope of gaining a first-hand knowledge of the Muslim situation, meet important personalities, stay in touch with the latest developments, and, may be, warn the participants of the dangers the Islamic world was facing from the Israeli-American conspiracies. They were attacking the already weakened Muslim of the world, and, with the help of the media and political influence, were trying to reduce the *Ummah*'s confidence in the *Shari`ah*, faith in its ability to solve its own problems, and create an inferiority complex among the muslims. Further, the new conditions had led to a situation of confrontation between the Muslim masses and their ruling classes: one for Islam and the other against, leading to wastage of energies in internal conflicts.

A little later, in May 1996, Ali Miyan found time to travel to Bombay, where he spent a whole month in a villa provided by a friend and follower, in the city suburb. In total seclusion, he engaged himself in editing some of his old works, writing the sixth volume of his "The Caravan of Life" being his own biography and, in some free time, listening to the first part of his own work "The Saviors of Islamic Spirit" read out to him. The next month, in June, he traveled to Bangalore and toured several South Indian towns, performing opening ceremonies of Madrasas, educational institutions and orphanages. Later that year he set off for Turkey to attend the annual meeting of the "Islamic Literary Association," (touching first on Dubai, delivering a speech to the Urdu audience there). In Turkey, Dr. `Abdul Mun`im Ahmed Yunus (Azahar University), Muhammad Qutb, Yusuf al-Qaradawi, Muhammad Ali Sabuni, Dr. Abdul Quddus Abu Saleh (Imam Ibn Saud University, Saudi Arabia), Dr. Hasan al-Imrani (Morocco) and others were also present. The main article of the session was on Ali Miyan himself, prepared and read out by Yusuf al-Qaradawi, "*Da`wah Principles in Abul Hasan Ali Nadwi's Writings.*" Seven more articles followed in later sessions. While in Turkey, he also thought it fit to send his customary letter to Najmuddin Arbakan, the Prime Minister of Turkey pointing out the need for creating Islamic awareness, especially among the youth.

The media was another element that, according to him, needed to be reformed. From Istanbul he proceeded to London to attend the opening ceremony of the Nadwah type *Madrasah* in Nottingham. Later he visited the Islamic Foundation in Leicester where professor Khurshid Ahmed, Khurram Murad, Manazir Ahsan (Director) and others received him and where too he delivered a talk. Returning to

India via the Hejaz where he visited Makkah and Madinah, he landed in Bombay and then traveled to Delhi to visit the Tablighee headquarters in Nizamuddin. It was to offer condolence over the death of Mawlana Izhar al-Hasan Kandhlawi, who was the chief of the Shura committee. By December he was in Hyderabad to attend a seminar on the "Islamic Literary Forum." In December too he was back again in the Hejaz to attend the Muslim World League's session on Mosques.

The Divisionary Forces

Early in the year 1997, a movement with its power base in the Gulf began to gather strength, seeking to discredit famous past Muslim personalities, present day scholars, institutions, and the *da'wah* movements that had sprung from the Indian sub-continent. The discrediting move against them was simply because they subscribed to the *Hanafi Fiqh*. Ali Miyan spoke out and wrote strongly in protest. This new movement pitched its tent against an *Ummah* in India that was already under pressure, if not on the run, and was behaving as if it was fighting infidels. The leaders of the new movement forgot who their common enemies were and what the true challenges that the Muslims were facing in this region. They ignored the writing on the wall that even if every individual Muslim began to sing their song, abandoning the local leadership and following those sitting far away, who had little interest or no understanding of the Indian situation, the problem of maintaining an identity as Muslims in this region would not be mitigated.

He felt that it was being locally pursued for financial advantages and externally incited for fanatical reasons. Those who had no past record of service to the *Ummah*, could only gain attention, credit and leadership, by first discrediting those who were in selfless service from the day Islam had set foot on the sub-continent. Ali Miyan wrote a long article highlighting the services rendered by the great scholars and movements of the past, the present-day efforts by individuals and movements, and the dangers in the efforts to divide the *Ummah* on fresh lines with the help of holy slogans. He got his article sent across to all those in the Arab world who mattered, adding up a detailed letter to ten well-known *Salafi* scholars pointing out the need to curb the efforts at declaring anyone who followed one of the four *Fiqh* schools as those committing *bid`ah*, creating a front where no front existed and fighting one's own brothers as one fights an enemy. In reply, Sheikh Abdullah bin Baaz - the grand Mufti of Saudi Arabia whose name was being used without his knowledge for strength and authority - wrote that "The Higher Council of Research and Religious Rulings" as well as "The Council of *Fiqh*" of the "World Muslim League" had already issued rulings that it was perfectly alright to follow any of the four well-known schools of *Fiqh*. The Sheikh also praised the work done by the founders of the four *Fiqh* schools. His reply carried the signature of several other scholars of Saudi Arabia. Other scholars also responded well.

Meanwhile Ali Miyan's friends in high places had not forgotten or forgiven him. The Lucknow edition of *"The Hindustan Times"* reported in its 22nd Feb. 1998 issue that while several terrorists had infiltrated into the country and were operating freely, the law and order authorities were sleeping. The terrorists named were: Abdul Mawdudi, Abdul Hasan Al-Nadwi, Dr. Abdul Hameed Qadri and Muhammad Manzur Noamani. (The slight twist in the names were, of course, accidental!) Despite a Muslim journalist informing the editor that of those named two were already dead, a third unknown, and a fourth an honored citizen and a true son of the soil, more patriotic than the most (fraudulent) patriots of the day. The newspaper took no notice. Then, in April the same year, the country offered him another gift. Local and foreign newspapers reported that a criminal case had been filed against Abul Hasan Ali Nadwi and some others, and a non-bailable arrest warrant had been issued by the Judicial Magistrate Ashok Kumar Singh. The charges? Ali Miyan and his accomplices had made off with huge amounts collected for Muslims affected by the attacks on their life and property during the 1995 Meerut riot. Those who had filed the case were "Muslims!" However, after some legal proceedings, the case was withdrawn and those "Muslims" disappeared.

Also in 1998 having just been back from the Hejaz he found the energy to make a full circle tour of the Indian cities in the north, central and southern parts. Then in August he was in Amman to attend the yearly conference of the "World Muslim League of Islamic Literature." Amman had, over the years, developed into a sprawling modern city. An interesting religious development was that all mosques had a radio which relayed the *Adhan* five times a day to the loudspeakers of the mosques. (The countryside was spared). Ali Miyan was well received by Prince Hasan, who arranged for a lavish dinner for the participants. Ali Miyan was also requested to record something for the television. In response he got recorded a talk. But, as luck would have it, according to the television authorities, the recording was so poor due to machine failure that it could not be broadcast! On his wheel chair, Ali Miyan visited the two holy sites in the Hejaz in his return journey.

Vande Mataram Again

Following the 1997 election when BJP was able to form government in the Center in coalition with other parties, the time had come to introduce in the schools a song known as Vande Mataram. It issued directives to all educational institutions that every classroom was to have a map of India and 400mmx700mm image of the Saraswati goddess. The students were required to gather before the map and the image and sing Vande Mataram. An approximate rendering of the song would be:

"You (O Land, and O goddess Saraswati), are my knowledge, my religion, my hidden, my goal, my internal soul and the strength in the arms. It is your reality that resides in the heart, and your idol alone. In every temple you are the Durga (goddess) with ten armed hands. You are the Kamala, the spring of the lotus flower. You are the water, that bestows knowledge. I am your slave, slave of the slave, slave of the slave's slave. O you of the sweet water, rich fruits. You are my mother. I am your slave. I salute mother Bharat."

The students were also required to garland the map and the image and stand a while before them in reverence and then, finally, sing the national anthem. Muslims of all classes opposed the introduction of the pagan practice. They could not be expected to go along with the practice when their Holy Book said,

"He is Allah, other than whom there is no deity, Knower of the Unseen and the Seen. He is the All-Merciful, the Benevolent. He is Allah, other than whom there is no deity, the Sovereign, the Pure, the Perfect, the Bestower of faith, the Overseer, the Exalted in Might, the Compeller, the Superior. Exalted is Allah above whatever they associate with Him. He is Allah, the Creator, the Inventor, the Fashioner; to Him belong the best names. Whatever is in the heavens and the earth is exalting Him. And He is the Exalted in Might, the Wise."

Could those who believed in a God of such attributes ever bow down to idols, deities, images, or the map of a country? No Muslim bowed down to the map of Pakistan, Malaysia, Saudi Arabia, Iraq, Egypt or Morocco. Muslims of all classes and regions were therefore completely opposed to the practice that the government wished to introduce. Ali Miyan issued a clear statement that it would be better to withdraw all Muslim children from the schools rather than accept the introduction of idol worship. Protests all over India, including by the Shi`as whose leader Mawlana Kalb Ali Sadiq said that the Shi`ah will not prostrate themselves even to Imam Hussain, far from idols. As a result of massive protests all over India the government was forced to retract.

Prime Minister Vajpai and home Minister Advani issued statements that originally the order had not been meant to be mandatory, although, copies of the original orders clearly showed otherwise and exposed the lies of men in high positions. Some newspapers reported that the orders were cancelled, meaning that at one time they had been issued.

Many things happen in India by co-incidence. It was by coincidence that in November 1998 representatives and correspondents of the Radio, T.V., newspapers and magazines, including the "BBC," "Star" and "Zee-T.V." inundated Nadwah. They all wished to interview Ali Miyan over the Vande Mataram issue. The reports of the interview and Ali Miyan's opposition to the introduction of Vande Mataram in schools also brought the security agents to Ali Miyan's residence in Takya Kalan. They chose 2 a.m. as the time suitable for their visit. They entered his guest house and made a thorough search. Nevertheless, not finding anything objectionable returned empty handed. Luckily Ali Miyan was then in Lucknow.

The spread of the news of the raid brought prominent men of politics and government to Nadwah in sympathy. Sonia Gandhi too wrote a letter to him expressing her deep concern at this kind of mean behavior against a man of global fame of whom the nation should be proud and whom the Nehru family had always deeply respected. The Rae Bareli public was also with Ali Miyan. A protest strike was called by Mr Akhlaish Singh and for the first time ever in the history of the city, shutters of every shop, small and big were brought down for twenty-four hours. Even little corner shops did not open.

If the security agents were raiding Ali Miyan's house in appreciation of his efforts to create peace and harmony in India, recognition came from abroad in a manner distasteful to them. In January 1999 he was awarded the "Most Prominent Islamic Personality" award by the "International Qur'an Organization" in Dubai. Unable to stand on his legs, he received the award on a wheel chair and distributed the accompanying amount among various educational and welfare organizations in India. A month later and despite increased weakness, he traveled to Bombay, Bangalore, Bhatkal and Bangalore to attend various functions. But when he returned in March he was exhausted. A stroke paralyzed the right wing of his body. It was decided by friends, followers, and relatives that he be taken to Delhi by chartered flight. The state government agreed to provide the aircraft. However, everyone was apprehensive of 'Ali Miyan's approval, since it was his known principle that he didn't accept any help from the government. As feared, when it was mentioned to him he protested strongly and the proposition was dropped. Although that was a setback for the several doctors attending him, he however, with quick and massive treatment began to show signs of recovery. From almost complete paralysis to movement of arms, fingers, the ability to write the *Basmalah*, stand up on his feet for a while, to finally move about a little: every week he showed improvement. In about two months he was able to deliver a half hour talk in the annual Tablighee gathering in Nadwah.

As the news of the stroke spread, visitors started pouring in from all parts of the country. One of them was the Saudi Ambassador. The other was the Prime Minister of India, Mr. Atal Bihari Vajpai along with the Chief Minister of UP and its governor. Ali Miyan told them that the only way India could survive as a nation was to follow the three golden principles that had kept its various irreconcilable elements together: democracy, secularism and non-violence. Mawlana Rabe` Nadwi, the rector of Nadwah, gave them the *Hadith* example of a double-decked ship. The hole that the lower deck travelers make if denied water by the upper deck travelers would sink both. The visiting party listened in silence and left in silence. What was the effect of the admonition was to be demonstrated a little later.

By June Ali Miyan had recovered enough to be able to move about in a wheel chair and - cancelling his journey to Bombay, to escape the heat of UP - he decided to stay back in Nadwah to address the Tablighee gathering being organized there. Speaking in a weak voice to the 100,000 delegates, he told them that the Muslims should build up such an exemplary character that people point their fingers at them and say, "There goes a Muslim, a slave of God, an exemplary person." It is individuals of this kind, when produced in large numbers that was likely to wipe out paganism, worship of false gods, and the inordinate love of wealth the contemporary society suffered. It was a matter of serious concern that in a country where such large number of Muslims lived, they were unable to bring about any moral change. It implied that they had not accepted the religion of Islam wholeheartedly. It was time that the Muslims improved not only upon their faith and beliefs but also attended to their moral rectitude, their social behavior, their worldly dealings, and everything else without any section of life left uninfluenced by Islam. Allah had commanded them to "accept the whole of the religion of Islam." A part acceptance, say fifty or eighty percent, did not meet with the requirement. Nothing less than hundred percent was acceptable. Muslims should return from this gathering with a firm resolution that as they spread out from here, all over the country, "they will live by Islam" - the whole of it. Their character and conduct in private and public should be such as that would influence the people around them. A revolution is necessary, but not political, rather within the individual's soul, and at mass level.

Many people were surprised that a man who could not ordinarily speak out a few sentences, was able to deliver a forceful lecture lasting twenty-seven minutes. He himself was surprised at the outpouring of energy.

A fitful response to his calls came two weeks later. A Hindi daily based in New Delhi reported that Ali Miyan had addressed a huge gathering of religious men and had incited them against the country, advising them to seek separation. The report alleged that he had also got distributed thousands of pamphlets that advised the people to spread out in the country and take the message of insurrection to its every nook and corner. The report also said that Ali Miyan was requested to pray for the soldiers fighting against the enemy in Kargil (Kashmir), but had refused.

Ali Miyan started receiving telephones, faxes and letters asking him to confirm if the reports were true. Lucknow University students, who share a wall with the Nadwah and who had always in the past pelted stones on Nadwah at the smallest pretext, issued the statement that they'd burn down Nadwah since all Arabic and religious Madrasas were terrorist organizations. On this particular occasion stone-throwing assumed severe proportions. Several political organizations, however, especially those who were in the opposition benches reacted firmly, protesting against allegations that were absolutely baseless. Many important non-Muslim senior politicians, social workers and intellectuals came down to meet him to express sympathy and solidarity.

But there was to be no peace between those who carry with them an open agenda against the Muslims, (wrongly referred to as the "hidden agenda"). When Ali Miyan was awarded the Sultan Brunei Award for his services to Islam, which was organized by the Oxford Centre, and a senior Minister of Brunei was to come down to Lucknow to present the award, since Ali Miyan was unfit to travel, the government of India refused the Minister's journey to Lucknow on grounds that it was unable to provide the necessary security to a foreign dignitary. (How could security be a problem when Sonia Gandhi had recently traveled to visit him in his sickness)? Finally, the Brunei High commissioner decided to hold the function at Delhi where Mawlana Rabe` Nadwi represented Ali Miyan to receive two shields and a cash award. This time, following the suggestion of a close associate Mawlana Abdul Karim Parekh, Ali Miyan decided to distribute the amount among his poverty stricken relatives. Mawlana Parekh also received a share for his good advice.

By now, Ali Miyan was confined to the wheel chair completely, praying from a sitting posture, at home, except for Friday Prayers which he insisted on doing in the mosque.

In October 1999 he received an invitation to chair the Muslim Personal Law Board meeting in Bombay. He couldn't go, but sent his address. It was his last public address. It said, "We Muslims have consciously decided to live in India. Nothing but Allah's own will can change our will to live here. This decision was not taken out of any weakness, rather after a careful consideration. Another of our decision is that we shall live in this country remaining true to our beliefs, Islamic laws, and following our own culture. We are not ready to make the slightest of compromise over these issues. And why not when as citizens of this country, we are given this right by the constitution? Having chosen to live here, it does not follow that we should do it at the cost of our holy law, religious instructions, beliefs and culture. If we did that, it would mean living not in a free land, but rather in a prison. It is true that our physical bodies are made from the soil of this earth, but our culture is Abrahamic, and wherever a Muslim lives, his culture will remain Abrahamic. We see no reason why we should live in this country as its second class citizens." A little later the seventh volume of his biography, written by himself (*Karawan-e-Zindagi*) came out of the press. It was his last written work. The book is a unique contribution. This writer doesn't know its equivalent in Urdu, English or Arabic. Although a personal biography, it reflects the conditions of the time, peoples, movements, institutions and individuals, spanning over almost a whole century.

So far, we have been writing on the public affairs of Ali Miyan. That is because he was a man of public. It was only for short spells that he stayed in his home town. He utilized that time for writing books. But visitors, telephones and faxes would not let him rest for long. A stream of invitations with accompanying tickets. It's time now we offered a few lines on his personal life and habits.

His Person

Personal Habits

His day started with *Tahajjud* prayers (somewhere in the last third part of the night). After the Prayers he busied himself with the recitation of the Qur'an and in *Dhikr* until the dawn prayer. *Dhikr* was vocal. After the dawn prayer he went for a walk. During the walk he either recited the Qur'an (most of the time *Surah Ya Sin*, from memory) or engaged himself in *Dhikr*. After returning he did his breakfast and then offered the *Ishraq* prayers. Thereafter he recited one-thirtieth part of the Qur'an. Some times he listened to the Qur'an recited to him. That over, either he sat down to pen down a new book, or attended to correspondence. That lasted until *Zuhr* prayers which was followed by lunch. Then he rested until about half an hour before *'Asr* when, having got ready for the prayers, spent the time reading. The time between *'Asr* and *Maghrib* (about an hour) was spent in the company of visitors. After *Maghrib* he offered the *Awwaabin* prayers spending an hour and a half reciting the Qur'an in Prayers. He also did some reading at this time. Dinner after *'Isha*, some chatting with friends and others, closed the day and he went to bed roughly by about 10. Sometimes, especially after 1977, he suffered from sleeplessness, turning about in the bed the whole of the night. When that happened he slept a couple of hours after daybreak. During his last years his recitation of *Surah Yasin* began to take longer time. On inquiry he explained that he recited this chapter 13 times everyday, and on one of the week days 14 times. It took two hours of his time. Starting with Abu Bakr and ending with the last great personality who worked for the revival of Islam, he bestowed on to them the rewards of the *Yasin* recital naming them one after another. He also named all those who served him, or had ever served him. When he entered a town, he entered reciting *Surah Ya Sin* and bestowing the reward of the recital to the dead of the town. On Friday he recited *Surah al-Kahf* without fail, and wrote a book dealing with various aspects of its meaning. Also on Friday, he spent an hour or more in supplications before the Prayers. He liked to repeat the Ta'if and 'Arafat supplicatory words of the Prophet.

He was very particular about what he consumed avoiding the unlawful and even the doubtful. Sometimes he went to dinner parties but returned having eaten nothing because he was not too sure of the lawfulness of the food. On occasions when he ate the unlawful unknowingly, his stomach rejected it. During air journeys he kept reciting the peace formula on the Prophet (*Salah wa Salam*). He remained in *Wudu* all the time and entered the mosque with the Prayer Call.

As long as `Abdul Qadir Ra'epuri was alive he spent most of the month of Ramadan with him. After his death he began to spend his Ramadan at Takya Kalan. In his early days he himself led in the *Taraweeh* Prayers for the first twenty *raka`ah*. A couple of hours later he did four more *raka`at* reciting some two of the thirty parts of the Qur'an. He also listened to one of the thirty parts of the Qur'an, from recorded cassettes of Qari Qasim. In the initial years, he had a hundred to two hundred men as his guests during Ramadan at Takya Kalan. But in his last years the number began to rise to several hundreds, reaching up to a thousand, whose food costs were borne by him.

Quality of Speech and Writings

Being a well-schooled scholar, master of words, he could tread the middle path, speak out his mind without committing an error, an exaggeration, or an underestimation. One can read through his entire works, without being able to place a finger on a statement that is incorrect, or on the extreme side, or overemphasized. Whether it was creeds, devotions, legal matters, social laws, or political thought, he took interest in all, and spoke with equal authority. He also knew the need in his times for someone to actually demonstrate the middle path, for he could see seeds of rightist statements sprouting into trees of extremism. When he was in a Tablighee gathering, he pointed out to them the material needs of the *Ummah*, while in Jamat-e-Islami assemblies he would talk of the need to look inward into the soul. It is said about Shukri that while in prison he read heavily two influential writers of the second half of the last century. One would be curious to know if he read Ali Miyan also.

An important quality of his writings and speeches was that he never hurt anyone's sentiments including even the enemies of Islam. He never criticized because he was angry, or disappointed. He never taunted because "they had not followed my advice." He was never bitter. In fact, he never criticized unless it was something important. This writer can remember that when one of his articles appeared in an Arab magazine, with the sum and substance that Indian Muslims were facing problems, without any details whatsoever, an Arab remarked, "Muslims must be facing very hard times there for Abul Hasan Ali to raise the issue." He was soft, subtle and indirect: entirely in the Arab style. Some of the audience could go back dissatisfied, but none in anger or alienated. Indeed, this is one important aspect of his approach that made him popular among all. Whenever there was a mixed gathering, of all kinds and classes, belonging to variant schools of thought or even sects, keeping whom together was important to the organizers, whether it was in USA or south India, the choice of the managing committee would fall on him for the key address.

Perhaps the following can be quoted as a latter day typical Ali Miyan speech. When a World Muslim League conference was taking place in Karachi in 1978, professor Ghafoor Ahemd hosted a dinner in his honor. The gathering was attended by leading political, social, and religious leaders of the country along with many leading personalities and press staff. Here he delivered a speech, whose ending part ran as follows:

"It might be attributed to my talent, or to my trial, a blessing from Allah or a test, I ca not say which, but I can say, with great respect for those present, that perhaps there is none here who has been able to see the world of Islam as closely as I have. It amounts to some bad luck for me as well as some good luck; bad luck because the way I have seen the world of Islam, has left a burning mark on my heart. It leaves a wound there. Good luck, because I have had the opportunity to see the Muslims from close quarters. In other words, I have had the chance to see parts of my own body.

"At all events, I would like to tell you that the question now is not that of belonging to this or that movement. It is not that of the momentary demands. It is that of the destiny of the *Ummah*. Maybe you feel sure you have the freedom in matters of worship. Maybe, you still have the freedom to do certain types of business following Islamic norms. But, the *Ummah* as a whole carries no weight in the scales of world politics. Whether the issue is Jerusalem, or Palestine, whether it is the Lebanon question or Cyprus. You can see that the whole Islamic world has no effective say. After the fall of the Ottoman Empire, there is no Islamic country, no group, no organization that can throw its weight in favor of an Islamic cause. King Faisal had shown some courage, and managed to pull some weight. But at present there is no Islamic country on the globe whose approval or disapproval matters, whose protest is paid attention to - even for a second - by any of the big powers.

"I would say you have to rise above party loyalties to face the situation. Accept the challenge that the contemporary world is throwing at you. Accept it with courage. Wait for an opportunity from Allah. When it comes, make the best of it. If you find any organization or movement with say ten percent of the ability that you demand of it, still use it. Your sincerity demands that you give its members the chance to prove their worth. Keep before you these lines of Muslim destiny. These are not for wall decorations. These are the lines of your destiny. Your minor mistakes, minor selfishness, minor provincial leanings, or factional support can cause confusion among you and differences can translate into considerable losses to the world

Muslims. Whenever you get that chance, give preference to the *Ummah*'s needs over your own. You should avoid every such issue, every such question that can create chaos in the Muslim society. If you have to keep some of your old disagreements away in a closet for a while, do it. It is binding upon you that you do not stoke such issues that divide the people. In fact, I believe if some of the religious movements had avoided this from the start, if they had set aside for a few days, discussions over minor issues, and unimportant questions, then, greater achievements were then possible, than what appears today. Nevertheless, those were, after all, human efforts and a person is only questionable to the extent of his understanding.

"I am sure you have understood the unspoken parts of my talk. That should be enough. I pray to Allah that He accept you for the world of Islam, indeed that of the entire humanity, as the guardians of truth, justice and equality. And that you rise to a status of the kind that no wrong can be committed in any part of the world, simply because of your moral weight.

"Today, the *Ummah* is in need of a 'Mu`tasim' – like the Abbasid caliph whom an old woman, captured by the enemies of Islam, called 'Ya Mu`tasima', and, in response, Mu`atism Billah sent an army to rescue her."

The above selection, part of a long speech has all the characteristics of his writings and speeches: He was forceful, but polite. He addressed major issues, choosing such as those that the time, place, or the makeup of the audience demanded. For every talk, he chose a new topic, and won hearing by presenting it in a creative style. (He often quoted extemporaneously Arabic, Persian and Urdu poetical pieces befitting the topic). He was there to remind. He talked in general terms, never went into details, and did not give the audience a program of action. For example in the above speech he was referring to the Muslim activists to teem up, and then wait for an opportunity to spring to action, even if the one to be supported has a fraction of the abilities they desired to see in them. His criticism was mild, indirect and he never mentioned persons or organizations by name to antagonize or alienate them. He made no specific demands on them. They went back, at worst, not too satisfied, but not too displeased either. He ended on a hopeful note, and encouraged the leaders to rise up to the need and the challenges of the time.

Also, he did not go into details of how things were to be done. He only pointed out the 'why of a thing' and the need for it. Means and methods were for the people to work out. He emphasized that given sincerity, with some margin of error, all efforts paid out in the end.
A recent book on Islam, written by a sober writer, in sober language, concludes, "The revival of the Islamic Community, as the Messenger had founded, though appears to be crying for the Moon, may, however, materialize in the form of the united states of the world of Islam with cooperation in defence, trade, industry and technology on the pattern of the present European Community and and it will be a new chapter in the history of the growth of the Islamic Community. If and when it comes into being, the Muslims of the world shall, only then, be liberated from the clutches of imperialism and assert themselves in the affairs of the world. It calls for jihad against their corrupt ruling class and its foreign masters whose stooges they are. Without it the change appears to be a remote possibility, only a romantic wish." (Professor Muhammad Yasin, "*A Glance At Islam*").

The above lines were written before the American invasion of Afghanistan and Iraq, and they are not of Sayyid Qutb, Mawdudi, or their likes, nor in fact of someone influenced by their thought. They are the words of an academician, a retired English language professor. They are the words of a former principal, and not of the hot headed students of his college. His level headed method of dealing with the question of Islamic revival throughout the book, reminds one of Ali Miyan's style, approach and spirit. But the concluding lines quoted above, set the two approaches apart. The writer of the story of Sayyid Ahmed Shaheed was completely opposed to this kind of talk. What was his own suggestion? It was to begin from below, from the individual, from the soul. Nobody could disagree with him. Indeed, even the ruling classes do not disagree with this "ideal" approach! They are far too happy if their subjects applied themselves to such an endeavour with all their energies, and of course, leave the affairs of the country, its economy, its natural resources, in fact, its honor, to them. They are confident they can undo in weeks, with foreign help, what the reformers achieve in decades. So, where is the middle line? Ali Miyan's writings and speeches do not seem to offer that middle line either, or maybe they do. Perhaps it is a question of outlook.

Asceticism

During his late years Ali Miyan had begun to earn unpopularity among a particular religious class of the Arab world. It could be in response to his criticism aimed at them. They spread the word that he had become a Sufi. Among certain people, brought up on hatred of Sufism – good or bad of it - that was enough to lower his esteem. Admittedly, he was a Sufi - in a sense: in that of asceticism, despise of this world, preference of the Hereafter, extreme humbleness, remarkable devotion to Allah, and other such ascetic qualities. For example, he never gave up his *'waza'if'* and *awrad'*, no matter what the circusmtance, whether traveling, or at home, whether in a conference hall, or in the corridors of a hotel. He never wished that anybody give him a special place in mind or heart. Once when he felt a sudden pain in his knee, Prof. Abul Khayr Kashfi (Pakistan) placed his hand on his knee. He reacted almost violently, "What are you doing?" he remonstrated. Abul Khayr told him that he was not trying to massage, rather, wished to read out some (holy) words and blow on them for relief. When he had done that 'Ali Miyan remarked, "It is a long time since somebody did that to me. Otherwise, normally people come to me seeking my blessings." He never sought the company of the renowned, especially if they were of the ruling class. When General Zia al-Haq sent word to him in Karachi that he would like him to visit him at Islamad, by a military aircraft ready to fly him, he replied that he had come to Pakistan after a long time, but for a short stay, and wished to give his kinsfolk the time they deserved. Finally, Zia took turn in asceticism by taking a flight to come down to Karachi himself. During the talk he asked him to suggest some *'waza'if'*. "You need to say the *'darud'* as often as you can,' Ali Miyan told him, and added, "but I suppose you should continue with your efforts," meaning, of course, "the efforts to Islamize the country." He was of course a critic of the perverted Sufism. He wrote about them:

"Those were professional exploiters of religion who, in addition, sought after fame. They were corrupt of belief. They in fact corrupted this religion and played a great role in perverting the Muslims and creating divisions among them. They used religion as a tool to free the people of Islamic obligations. In consequence, good Muslims discredited and ignored them. Some of these false Sufis were good of intention. But they were ignorant. For them the means were the ends, the body the soul.. Whereas, in sum and substance true Sufism is that whatever we do from morning to evening, following normal course of life, we do from a state of God-consciousness and in awareness that we are accountable in the Hereafter." He also produced a short work entitled *"Rabbaniyyah, la Rahbaniyyah"* (*Godliness and not Monkishness*). He did accept the *bay`ah* (compact of good behavior) of those who wished to enter into such a compact with him. But it was not a *bay`ah* of *Dhikr* or any of the well-known Sufi practices. The words of the pledge used to be, "I believe in Allah, besides whom there is no Lord worthy of worship, and in Muhammad who is His true Messenger. Hereby I abandon disbelief, association (with Allah), innovations, corrupt practices, and shall stay away from adultery, theft, unlawful wealth and slander. I shall do the Prayers regularly and give up the sins I have been committing. I also promise that I shall accept all of Allah's commandments and follow His Prophet. O Allah, forgive me my sins and inspire me to live a righteous life here onward."

After the pledge, he enjoined the following: 1) Hold fast unto *Tawhia*; 2) Follow the *Sunnah* as closely as possible; 3) Avoid all that is prohibited in Islam; and 4) Do three rosaries a day: i) of the testimony, ii) of the peace formula on the Prophet and iii) *Istighfar*. He was a Sufi in a few other ways also. One was his detachment from this world and attachment to the next. Poverty had been his lot from the birth. Once in his early life he happened to go to Hyderabad and had to meet a man of high position. Mawlana Manazir Ahsan Geelani (professor at Osmania Universty) was to take him. When he arrived in his long shirt and pyjamah, Mawlana surveyed him and asked, "Do you not have a *sherwani* (long overcoat)?" From the quick blush and confused movements he got the answer. So one was quickly borrowed. He traveled to places to deliver lectures or attend conferences. He did it at his own cost.

When the World Muslim League (Makkah) wished to fix an honorarium for him, his declining remark was, "Allow me to do something for the sake of Allah." Early on in Makkah he was regularly visited by Sheikh 'Umar b. Hasan, King Faisal's uncle, and president of religious affairs, with ministerial rank. Once he sent across forty Guineas as gift. (A Guinea was then equal to forty Saudi Riyals, an amount equal to about 25,000 dollars today). In about an hour Ali Miyan sent back the messenger with a letter to the Sheikh, accepting the gift, but only one fortieth of it, returning the rest with thanks and praises. In a second incident he was sent five hundred Riyals (a huge sum for those days) by Ameer Saud (the King's uncle). That was also promptly returned.

He never demanded to be paid for his books which were sold in millions. If a publisher sent him across some money, he accepted it. But he did not ask. Someone gifted him a new car. He refused to accept. The man was in tears so he conceded, "Alright, I accept it." But, after a few moments he told him, "Now accept it from me as a gift." On other occasions, when he was sent a car as a gift, he gave it away to Nadwah.

Similarly, all those gifts that arrived one way or another, were given away immediately to others. Never did he keep anything for himself. His wife too, treated the gifts sent to her in the same manner. Most of the award money was also given away in charity. In fact, he gifted almost everyone who came to him with something or the other.

Brought up in poverty, he did not banish it when better days arrived. Visitors to his house at Takya Kalan were offered tea in cracked teacups, sometimes with milk, which is the norm in India, at others a dark decoction without milk, which is a rare and considered a poor way of serving guests.

This total otherworldliness allowed him to criticize fearlessly. When he criticized Jamaluddin Abdul Nassir, the Egyptian President, a deity at home, he could not stomach it. He spoke to Jawaharlal Nehru (the then Prime Minister of India) to stop him. Nehru sent Badruddin Tayyibji to Ali Miyan, but he refused to budge. He was similarly fearless with criticism of the wrong, no matter from which quarter it issued.

He was a confident person and free of fear. Once he was waiting at the airport for a flight. It was delayed because of some mechanical problem. Someone who had gone down to see him off whispered in his ears that he had dreamt the previous night that the aircraft by which he will fly is fated to crash. He added, "This one is already having mechanical problems. So you better cancel the trip." Ali Miyan told him, "Do not speak of this dream to anyone. I shall travel by this aircraft and by Allah's will nothing will happen." His boldest stand was against Hindutwa movement. When singing of Vande Mataram (a pagan song) was declared compulsory in Indian schools, he warned the authorities that if they did not withdraw it, he will issue a *Fatwa* that Muslim children be withdrawn from all governmental schools. Finally, the song was withdrawn and the minister replaced. The various governments in India pressurized him several times to force him issue an statement against the Kashmiri struggle. But he never said anything more than that the Kashmiris had the right to determine their own future.

His writings: books, pamphlets, articles and published speeches, reach up the staggering figure of 700, almost ten for every year of his active life.

Standing Among the Scholars

Once as 'Ali Miyan had finished his *Tawaf*, Muhammad 'Ali Sabuni (the author of *Safwatu al-Tafasir*) met him and spoke to him for a while. While leaving, he narrated the following *Hadith* to his students, "Allah will not withdraw knowledge, withdrawing it from the breast of the scholars; but rather, He will withdraw knowledge by removing the scholars," and pointing to 'Ali Miyan he added, "He is of the *'Ulama* (scholars)."

One of Sheikh bin Bazz's secretaries, Sheikh Isma`il b. Sa`d, bin `Atiq remarked, "So and so writes with his brain. Sheikh Abul Hasan 'Ali writes with his soul. He is spiritual, devoted and sincere."
Teachers of the Saudi Training College produced a course book called "*Usul al-Tarbiyyah*" (Training Principles). Under a chapter titled "The Part Played by Muslim Scholars", the authors mentioned four outstanding scholars who appeared after the sixth century until today, who made sizable contributions: Badruddin Ibn Jama`ah, Imam Ahmed Ibn Taymiyyah, Abu Hamid al-Ghazali. The fourth named was Sayyid Abul Hasan Ali Nadwi.

Dr Khurshid Ahmed expressed his sentiments about him in the following words: "He had combined in himself the soul's longing of Dr. Iqbal, intellectualization and comprehensive concept of Mawlana Mawdudi, historical zest and *zenre* of Shibli and Sayyid Sulayman Nadwi, and the spiritualism of Ashraf Ali Thanwi, Mawlana Ilyas, Abdul Qadir Ra'epuri and Muhammad Zakariyyah. His true field was *Da`wah* and history of *Da`wah*, personality development, awakening of the soul, and the examples of the *Salaf* for the moral and spiritual upliftment of the *Ummah*. With him *Khanqah* and Jihad, purification of the soul and revolutionary changes, were currents of the same river..

I have personally profited both from Mawlana Mawdudi as well as 'Ali Miyan. I state the difference between the two personalities and their methiods in words, 'Mawlana Mawdudi entered into a person's minds by the routes of intellectual reasoning and then captured the heart, while Ali Miyan took the path of the heart to enter into the world of ideas and ideologies and refresh the soul.'"

The fact should not be lost sight of that no scholar was left in the last quarter of this century who had a pan-Islamic vision, who offered not simply a movement, but the whole of Islam, who stood in the middle, walked with everyone, knew and appreciated the efforts of all factions, divisions, and individuals. His *Ummah* was the entire Muslim world, in contrast to many whose claims contradicted their parochial attitudes and limited sphere of activities. Again, his view of Islam was overall. He never belittled political thought or activities, or economic efforts, or ascetic propensities. A traditional *Madrasah* or a modern school were the same to him: each served a function that the other did not. Both were essential, but both required a wider approach and broader spirit of accommodation. Similarly, people, all of them, with all their variety were the same to him: students, intellectuals, scholars, plebian: they were all equally important to the *Ummah*, and, therefore, all of them needed attention. Anything done for anyone, was for the benefit of all, and so, important to take note of, important to worry about. Therefore, individual were as important to him as the masses. Accordingly, he treated the individuals he met with equal respect, attention and fatherly kindness. It was keeping in with this principle that he would not listen to people's criticism before him.

Even when told that so and so had said offensive things about him, he smiled and changed the topic. Further, his own attitudes towards them did not change. He always wished them well, no matter what their own attitudes towards him. Once Abdul Majid Daryabadi criticized him strongly for refusing to be a substitute speaker to Mawlana Tayyibji Deobandi. But, he took it in good spirit, and remained to Daryabadi dutiful and respectful to the end. A few of his sayings

Western civilization creates means products but fails to offer a purpose for them.

Western civilization can never expected to be true and sincere with Islam and Muslims.

Knowledge is an indivisible unit. It cannot be divided into good, bad, eastern or western.

The Last Days and Death

Now we are with him in the last days of his life in the year 1999. As usual he wished to spend the month of Ramadan in his village Takya Kalan. Year after year, for some 20 years, people had been gathering there in Ramadan, sometimes numbering 400, spending their time in devotional acts. Sometimes, scholars delivered lectures. Shah Waliyullah's *Hujjatullahi al-Baligha* and his own *Al-Arkan al-Araba`ah* were also read out to the audience. Occasionally Ali Miyan also spoke. He also delivered the Friday sermons. However, this Ramadan doctors strongly advised against going to a village which did not even have electricity. So he visited the village before Ramadan. He met all the relatives, prayed in the old mosque, spent some time in its courtyard, went up to the bank of the river, looked around, and then went down to the family graveyard to pray for the dead. Finally, he entered his house where the womenfolk had gathered and sat with them for quarter of an hour. A little later he returned to Lucknow.

As Ramadan arrived, he did his first twenty fasts there. He also did the twenty *Raka`ah* of *Taraweeh* prayers every evening. Following his routine, he would rise for *Tahajjud*, do all his rosaries and *awrad*, recite the Qur'an and pray for his teachers, students and others. After *Fajr* and the activities that followed, he slept for a couple of hours. As he got up, once again he recited some Qur'an, and then met with the visitors, replied to letters, revised his works, and did some reading. When he met visitors arriving from distant parts, he inquired about religious activities in their town or country. He also inquired about the scholars of the area he knew, as to how they were doing. At times he listened to the Qur'an recitation. However, he needed other's help for his personal affairs, such as to take a bath, or move about a little. His brother's grandson Bilal and Haji Abdur Razzaq were always at his service. He was not very happy about this but there was no choice. At the same time he seemed to be aware that the time for departure had come: he himself half wishing it anyway. He would often say, "O Allah, unto You." Or he would say, "So, at last I am also to go. May Allah bestow a goodly reward." On occasions he would say, "O Allah, may You call me back. How long with these handicaps?!" To one of his attendants he said several times, "I have overburdened you. But a few days more." Nevertheless, the first twenty days of Ramadan passed well, with he doing things normally. Then he sought permission of his doctors to spend the last ten days at Takya Kalan, his ancestral village. Impressed by his energy, they agreed to the visit, with one or two of them deciding to accompany him. At Takya Kalan he remained normal for two days. As usual, a large number of followers had gathered for the yearly "*I'tikaj*." He asked about how many there were and was told that the mosque was full. "By Allah's grace," he remarked. He met many of them at his appointed hour of meeting. When his books came to be mentioned he remarked, "By Allah's grace were they produced."

On the second day he asked, "Is tomorrow the Farewell Friday (the last Friday of Ramadan)?" He was told that Farewell Friday would be on the day after. But he repeated, "Is tomorrow the Farewell Friday?"

On Friday, he got up at nine in the morning from his usual sleep after *Fajr*, offered two *raka'ah* of Prayers, did his usual rosaries, and completed other devotional acts. At 11 he took a bath for which he needed other's help, being partly invalid since the stroke. He wore his Sherwani (long overcoat) following his habit of never going to the Friday Mosques, or the Mosques of Makkah and Madinah without putting on the overcoat and socks. Then he sat down on his bed, and, following the practice (followed since he was eight years old) he should have begun to recite *Surah Al-Kahf*; but instead, he began to recite *Surah Ya-Sin*. It is not clear how many verses he recited since his voice was weak. But, a rough estimate is that he must have recited the first eleven verses:

"Ya Sin. By the Qur'an full of wisdom. Surely, you (O Muhammad) are one of the Messengers: on a Straight Path. (The Qur'an) sent down by the All-mighty, the All-merciful - in order that you might warn a people whose forefathers had not been warned, and so they are unaware. (However) the Word has come true that most of them will not believe. We have placed iron collars in their necks up to their chins so that their heads are high (up in the air). We have placed a barrier in front of them and a barrier behind them - thus We have covered them. So they do not see. And (therefore), it is the same unto them whether you warn them or do not warn them: they will never believe. You can only warn him who follows the Reminder and fears the Merciful - unseen. Therefore, give him glad

tidings: of forgiveness and a noble reward."

With those words his head rolled to one side. It was the last day of the century, and, his burial was completed an hour or so before midnight, just before the celebrations for the new millennium could begin. Swarms of people started pouring in from various directions and it is estimated that some quarter million prayed over him before burial. King Fahd of Saudi Arabia ordered prayers held for him in the Haramayn Sharifayn. It happened to be the 27th of Ramadan when the two mosques witness a collection of roughly three million devotees (5: 54): *"That is by the grace of the Lord. He accords it whom He will. And Allah is All-embracing, All-knowing."*

www.ingramcontent.com/pod-product-compliance
Lightning Source LLC
LaVergne TN
LVHW010342070526
838199LV00065B/5774